La

Strategies for Building a Joyful Learning Community

Susan Stephenson
Paul Thibault

Solution Tree

Cover art and design by Grannan Graphic Design, Ltd.

Text design and composition by T.G. Design Group

Illustrations by Tony MacKinnon

Printed in the United States of America

ISBN 1-932127-91-7

Acknowledgments

THANKS TO MY HUSBAND TOM and my family, who mean the world to me, and to the parents, students, and staff members in my career who inspire me to do my best and have fun at the same time—no matter what age we are. My deep gratitude goes to Monique Mili, my first humor collaborator and very funny friend, and to Paul for entering into unknown territory and writing this book with me.

—Sue Stephenson

I DEDICATE THIS BOOK TO MY WIFE, SHARYN; our sons, Peter and Jon; and my family for helping to make a dream come true. Thank you to my coauthor, Sue, and my many colleagues and friends who have shared their humor and laughter with me over the years and allowed me to share mine.

—Paul Thibault

We deeply thank Susan Chisholm who collaborated with us as our initial editor. She is a truly remarkable friend and a wizard with words.

Kudos are also due to Tony MacKinnon, the artist for the drawings that so aptly illustrate the spirit of each chapter.

We have made every attempt to credit sources accurately, but sometimes there is conflicting information about their origin. We welcome any information from our readers that will help us be more accurate in identifying original sources.

Table of Contents

Introduction

Having fun is not a diversion from a successful life. It is the pathway to it.
—Martha Beck,
life coach

IT IS NOT EASY BEING AN EDUCATOR these days. Many teachers and administrators work in competitive, isolated, and stressful conditions. Educators have spent decades trying to stretch dwindling resources. Newspapers publicize standardized test scores without any explanation of the complex factors involved. Administrative agendas conflict with union needs. Very little time is dedicated to professional development, and droves of teachers are retiring, leaving new teachers desperate for mentors. Collaboration is a commonly stated goal, but the culture and structure of schools often favor working alone. Creating an environment conducive to learning has become a much more complicated and sometimes daunting task.

And yet we still want to make our schools more effective for students—our hope and optimism continue. Without laughter and a culture of good humor to make continuous school improvement an enjoyable process, rather than an exhausting chore, we have little chance of achieving success—let alone sustaining it. Collegial, positive relationships among administrators, teachers, students, and parents are essential to securing collaboration and support from all stakeholders in the learning community. We must not assume that these relationships already exist. Rather, educational leaders must build and nurture those relationships, and humor is a valuable—and fun—way to establish connections.

The professional learning community approach to school improvement, for example, focuses on accountability, measurable results, and interventions, but a culture of distrust, low morale, and resistance to change often blocks teamwork and collaboration. The first step toward developing strong schools, therefore, is to create an atmosphere of hope, joy, and pride in one's work.

It is worth reflecting on what really lies at the core of the metaphor of "learning community." Consider these descriptions of communities:

> The PLC [professional learning community] framework can be grouped into three major themes . . . (1) a solid foundation consisting of collaboratively developed and widely shared mission, vision, values, and goals, (2) collaborative teams that work interdependently to achieve common goals, and (3) a focus on results as evidenced by a commitment to continuous improvement. (Eaker, DuFour, & DuFour, 2002, p. 3)

> A learning community consists of a group of people who take an active, reflective, collaborative, learning-oriented and

growth-promoting approach towards the mysteries, the problems and perplexities of teaching and learning. (Mitchell & Sackney, 2000, p. 9)

[A community is a] group of individuals who have learned to communicate honestly with each other, whose relationships go deeper than their masks of composure, and who have developed some significant commitment to rejoice together, mourn together and to delight in each other, make others' conditions our own. (Peck, 1987, p. 59)

The work that has been done to improve school effectiveness in recent years is impressive. However, we have never found any direct mention of humor and laughter in these theories. Almost 4 decades of working with educators in professional development workshops have convinced us that the use of humor and laughter heightens participants' attention, opens their minds, and increases their receptivity to change. Laughter opens the door to learning in large staff training sessions, in individual coaching, and in the daily life of a school.

This book is not intended to be a scholarly dissertation, but rather a practical, solution-oriented compendium of ideas gathered from our experience as teachers and principals. We do refer to a number of experts and current research, and we urge you to read further on the topics that intrigue you. From our experience, it is far easier to proactively create a collaborative culture than to reactively try to repair the damage of distrust and negative relationships—but it is never too late to build a joyful learning community.

We have always believed that leadership is an activity, not a position. Often, when people see the need for change in any school system, they focus on trying to change others. In our experience, however, the place to start is with yourself! Improved learning for students is the ultimate goal, but results for all staff, both individually and collectively, are equally important. Accordingly, this resource is intended for teachers, teacher-leaders, collaborative school teams, principals, assistant principals, staff developers, system-level administrators, and superintendents—anyone whose educational vision includes shared leadership.

The book is structured to examine how humor and laughter can create a healthier personal life, a dynamic classroom, and a stronger, more truly collaborative learning community. Feel free to jump to chapters that apply to your immediate needs.

Part 1 outlines the physiological, psychological, and sociological benefits of laughter, explores the connection between laughter and happiness, and provides examples of how you can nurture your sense of humor on an individual level.

Part 2 discusses the role of laughter and humor in learning and outlines practical ways that teachers can include humor and laughter in the classroom.

Part 3 shows how laughter and effective leadership fit together, provides specific strategies administrators can use to model good humor and joy within a learning community, and examines ways to use humor in professional development to increase the probability of true implementation.

As you read, share your reactions with colleagues. Reflect on how to apply these ideas to your own life, your classroom, your school or work setting, and your school system. Make a dedicated, conscious effort to promote the sound of laughter as a healthy sign of creative, eager minds and a strong learning community.

Chapter 1

Prescription to Laugh:
The Medicinal Importance of Humor

"Doctor, I have a ringing in my ears."
"Then don't answer!"
—Henny Youngman,
stand-up comedian

WATCHING A CHILD LAUGH is a truly joyful experience. Kids burst into laughter at even the simplest things. Humor guru William Fry found that "by the time the average kid reaches kindergarten, he or she is laughing some 300 times each day" (Doskoch, 1996, p. 35). Adults, however, laugh only about 15 times a day (Feinsilber & Mead, 1980, p. 60). Children seem to laugh a lot more and with an abandonment rarely seen in adults. When kids laugh, they put their whole bodies into it—not just their faces.

So what happens to this joyful exuberance as they grow up? We know that kids tend to become more serious and quiet as they progress through elementary school. They laugh and play less.

One reason is that Western society sends children subtle messages, often in the form of admonishments, about fun and laughter. How many times have you heard an adult order a child, "Stop acting like a child!"?

As busy adults, stressed by our careers and our families, we may think we have no time for fun. We lose our sense of playfulness. But taking charge of our happiness, banishing grumpiness, and actively looking for opportunities to recapture the joy of youth leads to significant health benefits.

HEALING THE BODY:
THE PHYSIOLOGICAL BENEFITS OF LAUGHTER

He who laughs, lasts.

—Mary Pettibone Poole, writer

Norman Cousins, a *Saturday Review* editor for more than 40 years, was the catalyst for pioneering research into the physiological benefits of laughter. During 1964, Cousins was being treated for ankylosing spondylitis, a debilitating, painful, and then-untreatable form of arthritis. Traditional medical treatments and the hospital atmosphere seemed to aggravate his condition, so with the approval and care of one of his doctors, Cousins took charge of his situation.

Cousins moved himself to a hotel, where he eliminated medications, except for large doses of vitamin C, and began watching humorous TV shows and movies with family and friends. The inflammation associated with the disease virtually disappeared, and he regained his health. He later reported, "I made the joyous discovery that ten minutes of genuine belly laughter had an anesthetic effect and would give me at least two hours of pain-free sleep" (Cousins, 1979, p. 39).

Since then, all kinds of benefits have been linked to laughter, some of them substantiated and some still under investigation. All researchers on laughter seem to agree on one thing: If you want to live better, laugh more. Laughter is free and accessible at any time of day. There are no negative side effects; even when we only *anticipate* a happy situation, we get a sense of euphoria, well-being, and balance.

The science of studying the biological benefits of laughter to our immune system is called psychoneuroimmunology. It is a rich field full of unanswered questions. Many articles assert that when a person laughs and is optimistic and joyful, the body reacts by secreting endorphins, the brain's natural painkillers, into the bloodstream. Others caution us that no studies have proven this claim (Klein, 2003b). However the body makes it happen, we know we feel better when we laugh.

What has been proven is that while we laugh and even into the following day, laughter increases the immune system's activity as measured by increased amounts of immunoglobulin G (an antibody) and complement 3 (which increases the effectiveness of antibodies) (Loma Linda School of Medicine, 1999). Other research shows that laughter

> activates T lymphocytes and natural killer cells, both of which help destroy invading microorganisms. Laughter also increases production of immunity-boosting gamma interferon and speeds up production of new immune cells; and reduces levels of the stress hormone cortisol which can weaken the immune response. Meanwhile, the perfect antidote others

have found that levels of immunoglobulin A, an antibody secreted in saliva to protect against respiratory invaders, drops during stress—but it drops far less in people who score high on a humor scale. (Doskoch, 2004, p. 34)

Specifically, a good hearty laugh:

- Increases oxygen to the brain and improves brain function

- Raises and then lowers heart rate and blood pressure (similar to aerobic exercise) (Klein, 2003a)

- Increases pain tolerance by distracting our attention away from intense pain and acting as a natural pain-killer (Provine, 2000)

- Massages internal organs and tones the abdominal muscles

- Loosens and relaxes the diaphragm and facial, abdominal, leg, and back muscles

- May prevent colds and upper respiratory problems

- May reduce the severity of infections

- Improves digestion

Some describe laughter as "inner jogging" and claim that laughing 100 times a day provides the physical benefits of 10 minutes of rowing (Fry as cited in Puder, 2003).

Laughter is currently considered a form of alternative medicine. Researchers continue to study the medicinal impact of humor and laughter on pain and on the immune function in diseases like cancer and HIV. Researcher Robert Provine advises, however, that "rigorous proof that we can reduce stress and pain through laughter remains an unrealized but reasonable prospect. While we wait for definitive evidence, it can't hurt—and it's certainly enjoyable—to laugh" (Provine, 2000, p. 61). At the very least, laughter is another healthy fuel for our bodies, much like sleeping, eating good food, exercising, singing, and dancing.

HEALING THE MIND AND THE SPIRIT: THE PSYCHOLOGICAL BENEFITS OF LAUGHTER

One laugh banishes a thousand worries.

—Chinese proverb

In today's world, negativity, loneliness, boredom, and burnout surround us. Laughter can help us escape these states, even if only for a few moments. Laughter and depression tend to be mutually exclusive. According to a study by Canadian psychologists Herbert Lefcourt and Rod Martin, people with a strong sense of humor become less depressed and anxious in stressful circumstances than people with a less developed sense of humor (Doskoch, 1996, p. 33).

Good humor lightens our psychic load. It refreshes the spirit, lessens pain, and makes us feel good again. Having a good laugh is like jumping into a swimming pool on a hot summer day.

In fact, the more tense, risky, and serious a situation is, the more we can benefit from a light-hearted moment in which we briefly ignore our problems. We can be silly and serious at the same time. Martha Beck describes this counter-intuitive truth in *The Joy Diet*: "The more stressful, dangerous, baffling or unpleasant your situation, the more important it is to laugh at it. The 'tickle' effect, the amount of hilarity produced by any given situation, seems directly related to how uncomfortable it makes us" (Beck, 2003, p. 156). Laughter harmlessly releases negative emotions like anger, sadness, and fear that have been stored up over time. After a tragedy, the first sign of healing is when people start to laugh again.

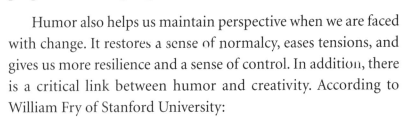

Humor also helps us maintain perspective when we are faced with change. It restores a sense of normalcy, eases tensions, and gives us more resilience and a sense of control. In addition, there is a critical link between humor and creativity. According to William Fry of Stanford University:

> Creativity and humor are identical. They both involve bringing together two items which do not have an obvious connection, and creating a relationship. (Doskoch, 1996, p. 34)

Teaching and learning are also about creating relationships and finding connections. We bring creativity to our teaching, so why not bring humor, too?

FORGING RELATIONSHIPS: THE SOCIOLOGICAL BENEFITS OF LAUGHTER

Something special happens when people laugh together over something genuinely funny and not hurtful to anyone. It's like a magic rain that showers down feelings of comfort, safety, and belonging to a group.

—Mary Jane Belfie, therapist

Although the physiological and psychological benefits of laughter are valuable, the positive social interaction that laughter brings to a learning community is its greatest asset. Most people are attracted to those who laugh easily and often. In our interactions with others, laughter acts like social glue and creates bonds that last for years.

Laughing softens a conversation. A well-timed funny comment can ease tensions and lighten the mood. Stress management consultant Loretta LaRoche says, "The most important thing I have learned is that laughter has the power to make us kinder to one another. When we're able to laugh together at ourselves, it truly brings us to a higher state of consciousness" (LaRoche, 2003, p. 85).

Consider these social benefits. Humor increases:

- Trust levels and willingness to discuss and work through real issues and problems

- Feelings of belonging and personal value to the group

- Enthusiasm, creativity, and productivity

- Teamwork and open communication

- Staff spirit, morale, and motivation

Humor decreases:

- Boredom and apathy

- Rivalries and conflicts

- Resistance to change

- Absenteeism rates and staff turnover

- Stress levels and visible tensions

MAKE A HEALTHY CHOICE

All organizations can benefit from a culture of camaraderie and support based on deeper relationships. If we doubled our laughs per day (LPD), the benefits to our health, our families, and our workplaces would be noticeable in a very short time. Laughter can help us physiologically, psychologically, and sociologically. Your own health as well as the health of your colleagues matters. Everyone benefits when you take conscious steps toward a more lighthearted and laughter-filled approach to life.

Points to Ponder

Far from mere reactions to jokes, hoots and hollers are serious business. They're innate—and important—social tools.
—Robert Provine, humor researcher

To what extent do you agree with our claims about the benefits of laughter on the body, mind, and soul?

How can you be more conscious of your LPD (laughs per day) and their effect on your mood and relationships?

Chapter 2

The Happiness Factor:
What It Is and How It Works

*Most folks are about as happy as
they make their minds up to be.*
—Abraham Lincoln

IS HAPPINESS MERELY THE RESULT of something extremely enjoyable, or does it hold deeper meaning? Can working in a true learning community lead to increased happiness and satisfaction in life? What do *you* think?

Take a few moments to reflect and jot down what you think the following words mean: "happiness," "optimism," "humor," "play," and "laughter." How do you think your close friends and family would define them? Understanding our own personal definitions of these terms can help us take a more positive outlook on life.

THE PURSUIT OF HAPPINESS

When America's founding fathers listed the pursuit of happiness as an inalienable right in the Declaration of Independence, they articulated one of humanity's most basic desires: to realize one's dreams and personal vision. Miles of self-help titles in bookstores across the United States and Canada—indeed, around the world—reveal our continuing obsession with this quest for self-fulfillment. "Happiness" is such a familiar word that we tend to take its meaning at a superficial level, but eventually, everyone discovers that it takes real and ongoing effort to define and pursue one's personal vision of happiness.

Americans in particular seem to approach everyday life in a positive way. A poll by *Time* found that Americans are overwhelmingly happy and optimistic, regardless of income. When asked if they were happy, 68% said that they were happy most or all of the time. When asked whether they felt they had lived "the best possible life . . . , a very good life, a good life, a fair life or a poor life," 83% responded that they had a good, very good, or the best possible life. Four out of five people polled said they wake up happy each day and consider themselves optimistic (Wallis, 2005, p. 43).

According to the poll, the major sources of happiness are:

- Relationship with children   77%
- Friends and friendships   76%
- Contributions to the lives of others   75%
- Relationship with spouse or partner   73%
- Degree of control over life and destiny   66%

- Leisure activities   64%

- Relationship with parents   63%

- Religious or spiritual life and worship   62%

- Holiday periods   50%
  (Wallis, 2005, p. 43)

How do these statistics fit with your experience? Do they surprise you or confirm what you already believe? The high ratings for children, friends, and spouses as sources of happiness reflect the social benefits of laughter and humor.

These results also remind us that having a sense of control over our own destiny is crucial to what we call happiness. John Morreal, president of Humorworks, says, "When we're stressed, we often feel like we have no control of the situation. We feel helpless. But when we laugh, at least, in our minds, we assume some sort of control. We feel able to handle it" (as quoted in Doskoch, 1996, p. 35). When we focus on how we can choose our attitudes, actions, and reactions, we feel empowered even in challenging times. When we focus on areas outside ourselves where we can have very little or no influence, we feel less satisfied and more stressed. Ironically, many people focus on these unchangeable areas. This "learned helplessness" creates the feeling that nothing you do matters; it often leads to depression, passivity, and demoralization.

THE EMERGENCE OF POSITIVE PSYCHOLOGY

Martin Seligman, former president of the American Psychological Association and the father of positive psychology, has spent 40 years studying the science of optimism and learned helplessness. Seligman founded positive psychology, he says, because:

I realized that my profession was half-baked. It wasn't enough for us to nullify disabling conditions and get to zero. We needed to ask, what are the enabling conditions that make human beings flourish? How do we get from zero to plus 5? (Wallis, 2005, p. 41)

Traditionally, counselors and psychiatrists have focused on what can be called negative psychology. They studied what caused their patients problems and tried to bring them from a negative state to a neutral, "normal" state. We now know that we can aim higher, for the positive emotions of joy and exuberance.

Figure 2.1 represents this idea graphically. Negative emotions such as pessimism, cynicism, anger, and anxiety are represented on the left side of the scale at -5. Positive emotions are shown at +5. Consider where you would place yourself and your school on the happiness scale.

Figure 2.1

THE HAPPINESS SCALE

-5	0	+5
miserable	neutral normal	joyful
down	not happy or unhappy	exuberant
depressed		fantastic

Can You Achieve Authentic Happiness?

Can we become happier people, or is our "happiness level" fixed at birth? One way to find an answer to that question is to consider Seligman's happiness equation: H = S + C + V (Seligman, 2002, p. 45), as Figure 2.2 illustrates. In his words, happiness includes "the idea that one's life has been authentic" (Seligman, 2002, p. 262). Being honest with ourselves and others, building positive relationships, and showing gratitude and forgiveness can create authentic, enduring happiness.

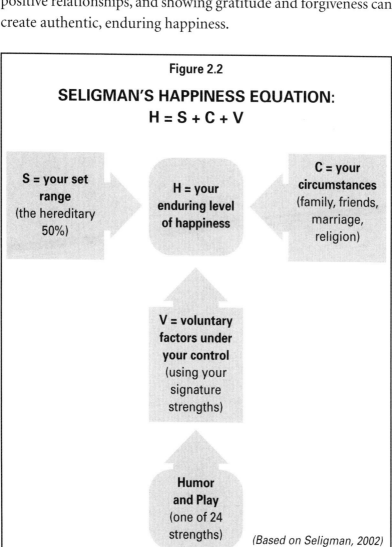

Figure 2.2

**SELIGMAN'S HAPPINESS EQUATION:
H = S + C + V**

S = your set range (the hereditary 50%)

H = your enduring level of happiness

C = your circumstances (family, friends, marriage, religion)

V = voluntary factors under your control (using your signature strengths)

Humor and Play (one of 24 strengths)

(Based on Seligman, 2002)

The *set range* (S) is what Seligman calls our genetic tendency toward a certain emotional span. Roughly half of our happiness potential is determined by hereditary factors. In fact, studies conducted on the personality development of twins and adopted children show that "the psychology of identical twins turns out to be much more similar than that of fraternal twins, and the psychology of adopted children turns out to be much more similar to their biological parents than to their adoptive parents" (Seligman, 2002, p. 47).

While some of our emotional tendencies may be predetermined by biology, we can change our external life *circumstances* (C) to increase our happiness—somewhat. Circumstances that contribute to happiness include having a healthy marriage, being part of a rich social network, believing in a religion, living in a wealthy democracy, and avoiding negative events and emotions. These circumstances are often hard to change, however, and account for only 8 to 15 percent of the variance in happiness (Seligman, 2002, p. 61). For educators, external circumstances may include factors like the socioeconomic level of the community, the personalities of other staff members, the union contract, the leadership styles of the administrators, and the current school culture.

The good news is that the many *voluntary* areas (V) or internal circumstances within our control are the most important determinants for how satisfied we feel about our past, how hopeful we are about our future, and how happy we feel in the present. For educators, voluntary factors include your attitude concerning the effect you think you can have on the direction of the school, your desire to make new relationships and get to really know the people on staff, and your commitment to the learning of all students, not just the most gifted.

This suggests that if you want to increase your happiness level, the first step is understanding that where and with whom you work are within your control. Sometimes that means changing the grade that you teach, interacting with different people in the staff room, getting involved with students in school activities, or consciously changing your attitude to feel more connected with the whole school. Becoming involved in school improvement on a collaborative team or in a study group offers a great chance to voice your opinions and disagree with dignity. If all else fails, you may need to look for a new school, a new district, or even a job in another field.

In these voluntary areas, we can use what Seligman calls our *signature strengths* to achieve our greatest level of well-being. He believes that to feel our highest degree of happiness, we must work with our unique combination of these 24 signature strengths.

Seligman has developed a strength survey, which is available on his web site (www.reflectivehappiness.com) and in his book *Authentic Happiness*. Taking the survey will help you identify your signature strengths—the ones most characteristic of the real you.

Keys to Happiness

"Humor and play" is one of the strengths that Seligman identifies. In his terms, humor is the ability to perceive, enjoy, or express what is funny or comical. Do you think humor is one of your signature strengths? Could you work on making it a more authentic part of your life?

THE 24 SIGNATURE STRENGTHS

Wisdom and Knowledge
1. Curiosity
2. Love of learning
3. Judgment
4. Ingenuity
5. Social intelligence
6. Perspective

Courage
7. Valor
8. Perseverance
9. Integrity

Humanity and Love
10. Kindness
11. Loving

Justice
12. Citizenship
13. Fairness
14. Leadership

Temperance
15. Self-control
16. Prudence
17. Humility

Transcendence
18. Appreciation of beauty
19. Gratitude
20. Hope
21. Spirituality
22. Forgiveness
23. Humor and play
24. Zest

(Seligman, 2002, p. 159)

Playfulness may be the most important component in determining and maintaining a sense of humor. Play is the expression of childlike qualities of inventiveness, curiosity, and excitement. It describes not what you do, but how you *approach* what you do.

Some of us never lose the capacity to play; others learn to suppress this vital ability as they grow older. Lighthearted play is often discouraged or forbidden in schools and workplaces for fear that the atmosphere will lack the serious tone needed to learn or be productive.

In reality, play brings out our human qualities and helps us to collaborate and create. Many people find they can innovate and solve complex problems better while they are having fun. Sometimes taking a moment to laugh clears the mind and makes the next steps in a task seem easier. When a group or class can play and work at the same time, they develop a deeper trust and form a stronger team. These are key aspects of a healthy learning community.

Inauthentic Happiness and Faux Fun

There is no correlation, Seligman says, between authentic happiness and financial or social standing. People who think the accumulation of material things and accomplishments will bring lasting happiness find no satisfaction. They take for granted what they once strived for and raise their expectations accordingly.

Authentic happiness has three components:

- The *pleasant* life—moment-to-moment pleasure, such as a great meal

- The *good* life—engagement in work, play, or relationships

- The *meaningful* life—the use of our signature strengths to contribute to something greater than ourselves (Seligman, 2002, p. 13)

People who find satisfaction in all three components stand the best chance of achieving lasting happiness. To lead an authentically happy life, Seligman suggests, we must use our signature strengths every day in our jobs, in our hobbies and volunteer work, with our families and friends, but most of all within ourselves.

Author and life coach Martha Beck makes another important distinction, between what she calls "faux" fun and real fun (Beck, 2002). Faux fun uses humiliation, ridicule, and mockery to get a laugh at the expense of others. This false sense of superiority, used to inflate our own egos while we laugh at someone else, is a less obvious form of prejudice. Unfortunately, many jokes use this harmful humor by stereotyping certain occupations, gender traits, countries, or ethnic groups.

Authentic fun is positive and encouraging. Think of fun times with your best friends: You connect with each other as equals and build memories, maybe over a great meal or during a special activity. The same is true of joyful learning communities: Collaboration involves great conversations, meaningful activities, and lots of smiles—maybe even laughter—all with the goal of making a difference in students' lives.

THE DIFFERENCE BETWEEN FAUX FUN AND REAL FUN

1. Faux fun helps you ignore problems; real fun helps you face them.

2. Faux fun gets boring; real fun never does.

3. If you're having real fun, you'll never regret it.

4. Faux fun makes everyone feel worse; real fun makes everybody feel better.   *(Beck, 2002, pp. 225–226)*

THE POWER OF A SMILE

The smile may well be the cornerstone of social interaction.
—Edward Philips, dentist

Smiling occurs regardless of culture, and as Darwin said best, we all smile in the same language. Children born blind instinctively know how to smile. Smiling is really a gentle, silent form of laughter.

Smiles are a subtle way of connecting with another human being. People who do not smile or have an unsmiling facial expression seem unresponsive, aloof, or angry. It is much harder to read a non-smile. Mannerisms offer some clues, but observers need to work much harder to decipher the message.

When people smile at us, they appear to be friendly and happy, and we respond to them more positively. When we smile at people who look unhappy, they often respond in kind, and everyone feels more energized. In fact, what we do with our facial expressions has a significant effect on how we feel even if no one is around. When we smile, the brain actually thinks about happy feelings, and our attitude changes—even if the smile is forced!

There are two kinds of smiles: genuine and fake. Each has millions of different meanings around the world. We learn to observe mannerisms and read the nonverbal messages accurately.

The movements involved in genuine smiling are involuntary. When you find something funny, 15 facial muscles contract, and the zygomatic major muscle around your mouth pulls up the corners of your lips. The muscles around your eyes raise your cheeks up, and the corners of your eyes crinkle. This genuine smile is known as a Duchenne smile, after its discoverer Guillaume Duchenne. It is a unique sign of positive emotion.

A fake or calculated smile, sometimes called the Pan-American smile (after flight attendants in TV ads for the once-operational airline), has none of the Duchenne features and can be seen as inauthentic. However, there are times when faking a smile and tricking our minds into thinking we are happy can get us through troubling times. The adage "Fake it 'til you make it" has some merit on occasion (Seligman, 2002, p. 5).

Smiling has a powerful effect on our willpower and confidence. When we practice positive self-talk and smiling, we go a long way toward achieving our goals.

MEASURING LAUGHTER

The positive strength of being humorous makes the state of laughing more likely.
　　　　　—Martin Seligman, founder of positive psychology

Laughter is a physiological response to humor that includes a sound and a set of gestures. When you laugh, the brain instructs you to produce both at the same time. During a real "belly" laugh, changes happen in other parts of the body, too, including the arm, leg, and trunk muscles.

We developed the Laugh-O-Meter (Figure 2.3) to illustrate the spectrum from a slight smile to laughing so hard that you cry. When you are laughing very hard, it is often difficult to get your breath, and your face can perspire and turn red. In extreme circumstances, the tear ducts open up in response to strong emotion. Crying releases toxins and brings relief.

Listen to the sounds of laughter in your school hallways and classrooms. Do certain people have signature laughs that can be identified by their unique sound alone? What does your laugh sound like? Use the Laugh-O-Meter to rate the intensity of the laughs you experience. How many belly laughs have you had lately?

Figure 2.3

THE LAUGH-O-METER

Crying

Belly laugh

Guffaw

Snort

Cackle

Chuckle

Giggle

Snicker

Full smile or broad grin

Twinkle

Slight smile

No response—default position

Negative response

Real-World Research

Robert Provine, a neuroscientist at the University of Maryland, observed the laughter of 1,200 people in their natural settings. Until his study, most research on laughter had been conducted in a laboratory.

Provine made three particularly relevant findings. First, the speakers laughed about 50% more than their audiences. This suggests that when we make jokes, our anticipation of others' reactions is important to our enjoyment. Second, ordinary comments and sayings such as, "Where have *you* been?" were more likely to prompt laughter than jokes; *people* are funnier than jokes. Finally, "laughter was 30 times more frequent in social than solitary situations," which again seems to suggest that laughing is often a social activity (Provine, 2000, p. 58).

We know without any formal research that just seeing someone else laugh can often make us laugh—even if we are not in on the joke!

An International Laughter Experiment

In September 2001, people from all around the world began visiting LaughLAB on the Internet to submit their favorite jokes and describe what they thought was funny about other people's submissions. Created by Dr. Richard Wiseman and sponsored by the British Association for the Advancement of Science, this unique experiment aimed to find the world's funniest joke and to answer important questions about the psychology of humor.

LaughLAB received thousands of jokes, and hundreds of thousands of people evaluated them using a special "Giggleometer" with a rating scale from 1 (not very funny) up to 5 (very funny).

As part of the LaughLAB project, scientists performed brain scans on people listening to some of the best jokes (see Appendix A, page 119). The results showed that a very precise area of the brain, the prefrontal cortex, plays a vital role in the type of flexible thinking needed to understand a joke. This result fits with other research suggesting that people who have damaged this part of the brain often lose their sense of humor, especially when the humor is based on incongruity.

The incongruity theory says that humor occurs when things that do not normally go together coincide: We expect a logical sequence and are amused when the illogical happens instead. Then, a split second later, we realize that there is a double meaning, and we laugh with surprise. This form of humor can be found in simple jokes as well as in very complicated stories: "Incongruity can take the form of contradiction, understatement, exaggeration, surprise, reversal, ludicrous or the totally unreal. . . . This theory emphasizes the mental or intellectual components of humor" (Shade, 1996, p. 10).

Consider some of these incongruous analogies from a widely circulated e-mail (allegedly collected from high school English essays):

- She had a throaty, genuine laugh, like the sound a dog makes just before it throws up.

- The little boat gently drifted across the pond exactly the way a bowling ball wouldn't.

- Her face was a perfect oval, like a circle that had its sides compressed by a Thigh Master.

- He was deeply in love. When she spoke, he thought he heard bells, as if she were a garbage truck backing up.

- Her vocabulary was as bad as, like, whatever.

Two other key theories of humor include the superiority theory and the relief/release theory. According to the superiority theory, we like to laugh at others when their mistakes, appearance, stupidity, or misfortune make us feel superior. This kind of humor is often prejudicial: Usually someone is being humiliated, embarrassed, or stereotyped. Students need to learn quickly from teachers that these "jokes" are unacceptable.

Relief humor offers a release from tension or stress, especially in scary or dangerous situations. Comic relief is often used to make fun of institutions we love to hate and to defuse uncomfortable topics like sexuality and death. Consider this example:

> An 8-year-old girl went to her dad who was working in the yard. She asked him: "Daddy, what is sex?" The father was surprised that she would ask such a question, but decided that if she was old enough to ask the question, then she was old enough to get a straight answer. He proceeded to tell her all about the "birds and the bees". When he finished explaining, the little girl was looking at him with her mouth hanging open. The father asked her: "Why did you ask this question?" The little girl replied: "Mum told me to tell you that dinner would be ready in just a couple of secs." (British Association for the Advancement of Science, 2002, p. 114)

SEEK SATISFACTION

For many of us, our biggest personal challenge is, "How can I enjoy each of life's fascinating stages and feel happier and more satisfied?" Researchers continue to take this question seriously and offer new insights into how we can pursue happiness more meaningfully. You can conduct your own research, too! Continued reflection on what makes you happy will increase your satisfaction with your personal and professional life. The next chapter will show you how to take action to increase your happiness level.

DO ONLY HUMANS LAUGH?

Over 2,000 years ago, Aristotle speculated that humans were the only creatures that actually laugh. There seems to be no truth to the belief that hyenas laugh. But some studies with rats and mice showed that they were more likely to learn new tricks if they were rewarded by being rolled over and tickled when they did well. The sound they made, called ultrasonic vocalization, was like giggling. Studies of gorillas and chimps have shown similar results, but many scientists today would agree with Aristotle that it is uniquely human to respond to funny situations by laughing out loud—especially when conducting experiments by tickling mice.

Points to Ponder

Smile for You

Smiling is infectious; you catch it like the flu.
When someone smiled at me today, I started smiling, too.
I passed around the corner, and someone saw my grin.
When he smiled, I realized I'd passed it on to him.
I thought about that smile, then I realized its worth—
A single smile, just like mine, could travel round the earth.
So if you feel a smile begin, don't leave it undetected.
Let's start an epidemic, quick, and get the world infected!

—Author unknown

Do you think humor is one of your signature strengths, or one you would like to develop?

Keep a journal of what brings you authentic happiness.

Chapter 3

Nurturing Your Own Sense of Humor

This is as far from trivial and self-indulgent as you can get. It may be the biggest and bravest thing that you do.
—Martha Beck

A FEW YEARS AGO, after one of our workshops for school managers, a woman quietly took us aside and asked how she could develop a better sense of humor. She realized that she needed help—a big step in her personal growth. Having a sense of humor is crucial to success and happiness, and thankfully, she knew it.

Many people believe that having a sense of humor means being able to spontaneously tell funny jokes. This is the furthest thing from the truth. There are many other ways to express humor. So slow down, relax, and with help from us, consider what suits you and your style.

CHECK YOUR FUNNY BONE

To figure out what will work best for your sense of humor, ask yourself a few questions:

- Do I have a great sense of humor already? Do I use it to make myself and others happier?

- Did I somehow lose my sense of humor? How could I get it back?

- Do I lack a sense of humor altogether? Do I want to change?

- Do my colleagues and coworkers think I have a sense of humor? Do they think I am fun to be with? How about my family and friends?

If you feel that you have never had any fun in your life and you do not even know where to start, see a doctor for a medical checkup or a counselor to talk about what is troubling you.

Most people only need some fine-tuning of their funny bone. Even the funniest people look for ways to hone their skills. With a little thought and effort, most people can raise their level of happiness and make daily life more fun.

BE YOURSELF

The whole object of comedy is to be yourself, and the closer you get to that, the funnier you will be.

—Jerry Seinfeld

All of us have a personality and a temperament that influence our unique sense of humor. What makes one person laugh hysterically may not be funny to someone else. Some people prefer visual humor like impressions and mime, while others are drawn to verbal forms of humor such as riddles, jokes, and anecdotes. The key to making people laugh is to always be yourself. Everyone can succeed with humor, each in his or her own way.

Martha Beck calls the pattern of activities you enjoy most your "funprint." Like your thumbprint, your funprint is unique:

> Each of us is born with a propensity to have fun doing certain types of activity, in certain proportions—you may love doing something I hate and vice versa. It seems obvious to me (and research backs me up) that we are most productive, persistent, creative and flexible when we're engaged in precisely the combination of activities that brings us maximum fun. Your funprint isn't a frivolous indulgence. It is the map of your true life, an instruction manual for your essential purpose, written in the language of joy. Learning to read and respond to it is one of the most crucial things you'll ever do. (Beck, 2002, p. 224)

Your funprint is intensely personal. Do not try to copy someone else or to force yourself to like a certain type of humor. Explore all the choices available, and you will know when you hit the right mixture to suit your personality.

Humor Temperaments

One way to explore your funprint is to examine it through the lens of temperament—a unique pattern of behaviors, talents, core needs, and values formed by a combination of your inborn characteristics and life experiences.

The study of personality or temperament types goes back centuries. As far back as 450 BC, Hippocrates identified four dispositions that he called humors: sanguine, choleric, melancholic, and phlegmatic. Each "humor" corresponded to a body fluid and described a personality type. The sanguine disposition, for example, was found in the blood and was considered impulsive and excitable.

This pattern of four types is also found in other theorists' work. Plato described rationals, guardians, artisans, and idealists. Aristotle studied which temperament made people happiest: dialectic, proprietary, ethical, or hedonic. Carl Jung examined eight cognitive processes people use to become aware of things and make decisions.

Many applied practitioners continued the work of defining temperament or personality types through the modern era. Isabel Myers and her daughter-in-law Katherine Briggs built the Myers-Briggs Type Indicator (MBTI) based on Jungian types. The MBTI was the first self-reporting assessment and made type psychology accessible to the mainstream.

In 1978, psychologist David Keirsey used Plato's four temperaments to create the Keirsey Temperament Sorter. His book *Please Understand Me* (Keirsey & Bates, 1978) became an instant best seller (visit www.keirsey.com for an online self-report instrument). Don Lowry, a California school teacher, expanded Keirsey's work to create True Colors®, which further introduced this notion of personality types to millions more, including many teachers and students across Canada and the United States.

One of our favorite temperament sorters is Personality Dimensions®, a Canadian self-assessment tool based on the work of Keirsey, Lowry, and Linda Berens, a student of Keirsey. Like True Colors, Personality Dimension uses colors to make four temperament types visual and accessible (Berens, 2000). We have conducted informal research to establish a relationship between the personality temperaments identified by Personality Dimensions and what we would call "humor temperaments" (see Figure 3.1, pages 38–39).

One of these temperaments will fit you the best and seem most natural, but you will find that you also have some proportion of the others. No single type is any better than the others; they are just different. Which combination of these four do you think you have?

Determining your personality type can be exciting: "Once people find their true temperament pattern, they experience a rush of energy and delight in knowing who they are" (Berens, 2000, p. 18). Knowing who you are can also help you to explore and nurture your own sense of humor as well as to appreciate the humor of others.

Schools and staff groups have used Personality Dimensions to profile the temperaments within the group or team. This requires great sensitivity to ensure that the group shows respect for *all* types. When a team knows its own unique profile, the group can achieve major breakthroughs in understanding what motivates each person, how each approaches conflict, and the unique contribution he or she can make to the success of the project and to the group as a whole. Looking at Personality Dimensions leads to great discussions about the temperament of a classroom, too; each class is full of unique personalities that need to find a successful place as learners.

Figure 3.1	
Personality and Humor	
Personality Dimensions temperament: Inquiring Green	**Personality Dimensions temperament:** Organized Gold
Core need: Knowledge and competence	**Core need:** Belonging through duty and responsibility
Characteristics: Logical, rational, investigative, systematic, clear-thinking, and emotionally self-controlled	**Characteristics:** Responsible, practical, loyal, helpful, and trustworthy; has a sense of right and wrong; maintains traditions and order
Humor temperament: Dry Wit	**Humor temperament:** Straight-Faced
Laughs at: Satirical, irreverent, political humor; clever puns and oxymorons; funny lists and slogans	**Laughs at:** Funny scenarios with details; a joke told well with a point; likes the social aspect of humor; prefers hearing to telling a joke
	(continued)

THINK FUNNY

Life coach Martha Beck advises us to make sure that we laugh at least 30 times every day; she calls this our LPD (laughs per day). Since the average LPD for adults is around 15, she suggests we try

Figure 3.1	
Personality and Humor (continued)	
Personality Dimensions temperament: Authentic Blue	**Personality Dimensions temperament:** Resourceful Orange
Core need: Relationships and self-actualization	**Core need:** Freedom, activity, and variety
Characteristics: People-oriented, sensitive, sincere, and supportive; relates well to others; seeks and appreciates harmony	**Characteristics:** Quick witted, funny, stimulating, creative, practical, risk-taking; seeks change and action
Humor temperament: Soft Touch	**Humor temperament:** Impulsive Entertainer
Laughs at: Warm-hearted, nonhurtful, self-deprecating humor; personal stories	**Laughs at:** Spontaneous, original humor, astute observations, improvisation, fast-paced zingers, bizarre situations

for twice the laughs we usually get (Beck, 2003, p. 158). There are many ways to "think funny." Some of our favorite ways to explore the funny and joyful side of life follow.

Rediscover Your Inner Child

Try to remember what made you happy as a child. Was it cartoons on television, dancing throughout the house to your favorite music, or ringing the bell on your bicycle? Ask your family about their memories of you. Reflecting on your childhood may remind you of the playfulness you may have lost growing up. Try to be more open to doing and expressing what the adult in you may perceive as childish, silly, or even outrageous. Go to a dance club and dance like you did as a teenager. Instead of watching your child or grandchild on the merry-go-round at the fall fair, get on yourself! Eat some cotton candy. Let yourself laugh.

Take Control of Your Attitude

Optimists do better in school, win more elections and succeed more at work than pessimists do.

—Martin Seligman

As chapter 2 discussed, positive psychology focuses on what really works for us and makes us happy. Once you determine what makes you happy, the proponents of positive psychology advise, just do more of that! Instead of living a life of regret, focus on what you have to be thankful for. What brings a smile to your face? What is special to you: eating great food, dancing to your favorite music, or riding a rollercoaster?

You feel how you think, so be aware of messages you send to yourself. Start each day with a positive attitude. The international consultant and lecturer Loretta LaRoche tells her audiences that when she wakes up in the morning, she looks in the mirror and exclaims to the world: "Ta da! I'm back!" This type of affirmative approach can change the outcome of your day.

There is real power in a smile. Even when you do not feel happy at first, just pushing up your cheeks and putting on a smile relaxes you and communicates warmth and trust to others. Smile, and the world smiles back. Your body and brain do not know the difference between a real and a fake smile. It may seem impersonal, but actively *choosing* a positive attitude really works to change your own mood and the mood of others around you.

Take Stock of Your Fun Quotient

If your work is making you stressed, try this sorting exercise from Ann McGee-Cooper to determine your "fun quotient" (McGee-Cooper, 1990, p. 78). Make a chart similar to the one in Figure 3.2, and write down as many fun activities under each time duration as you can.

Figure 3.2			
Sample Fun Quotient Chart			
2–5 minutes	**5–30 minutes**	**30 minutes– 1 day**	**1 day or more**
Reading the comics	Watching a sitcom	Going to a movie	Going to Disney World

How long did it take you to make your list, and how many items are on it? Most busy adults run out of ideas after listing between 10 and 15 items, but 10-year-olds easily generate 55 ideas in the same amount of time (McGee-Cooper, 1990, pp. 78–79).

If most of the activities you list need 30 minutes or more to do, how likely are you to actually get the time to do them? Try focusing on the ones that take smaller bits of time. Often these are less expensive as well as easier to schedule. You could also rate each activity on a scale of 0 (not much fun) to 10 (the most fun). What fun score would you give each of the activities you listed? By building fun into your regular day—even short chunks of it— you will be surprised at your increased energy and happiness.

Assess the length of time that your learning community devotes to fun. You may find that the key missing ingredient is laughter. Make building a *joyful* learning community a topic of conversation, and watch change begin.

Search for Funny Entertainment

There are whole industries built around laughter, and you can find lots to laugh at if you look for it.

If you are in the habit of watching serious dramas, consider watching **television comedies** like *The Daily Show With Jon Stewart, Frasier, Everybody Loves Raymond, Will and Grace, The Rick Mercer Show, Corner Gas, This Hour Has 22 Minutes,* or *The Air Farce.*

Check out the humor section at libraries and bookstores for **funny books** like *Made You Laugh: The Funniest Moments in Radio, Television, Stand-up and Movie Comedy* (Garner, 2004). Look for cartoon collections like Bill Watterson's *Calvin and Hobbes,* Gary Larson's *The Far Side,* or Scott Adam's *Dilbert.*

Look for **videos** by Jerry Seinfeld, Lily Tomlin, Bill Cosby, or another stand-up comedian. Choose funny **movies** like *Monty Python and the Holy Grail, Tootsie, As Good As It Gets, Fargo,* or your own favorite. Listen to **CDs** like Mike Nichols and Elaine May's *In*

Retrospect or Woody Allen's *Standup Comic*. See Appendix B, page 121, for more suggestions.

Write Your Own Sitcom

If your life feels like a drama, turn it into a comedy! Make up a title and choose the cast, director, producer, stunt actors, make-up and hair styles, wardrobe, music, and lyrics. What would you title your comedy sitcom? Have a laugh as you continually rewrite the script and plot lines.

Tell Stories About Yourself

A person who knows how to laugh at himself will never cease to be amused.

—Shirley MacLaine, actress and author

You do not have to be a Jim Carrey or Robin Williams to make people laugh and relax. Award-winning speaker Allen Klein (a.k.a. "Mr. Jollytologist") reminds his audiences that most people are not trying to become comedians; we are simply seeking humor for balance and perspective.

Telling jokes comes easily to some people, but humor can fall flat when the joke teller is uncomfortable or insincere. What tends to be more successful, because it is genuine and real, is to tell personal stories or anecdotes—especially those in which you can laugh at yourself.

For example, at one of our workshops, Sue told the following story. At her school, she explained, teachers had a tradition of celebrating the first 100 days of the school year with the first-grade classes. This event had always been a big success, and the teachers usually organized many special activities. During a recent celebration, she decided to dress up as the 100-Day Princess and meet the students as they were coming in from recess. She wore a pink feathered tiara, large glasses with the number "100" outlining the lenses, and a pink satin floor-length dress with puffy sleeves and a crinoline. Her wand made a magical sound when it touched anyone. One little boy looked up at her as he passed and said, "Is that what you look like when you are 100 years old?"

When Sue related this story to the workshop audience, hilarity ensued. By sharing her own embarrassing moment, she succeeded in bringing laughter to her listeners and herself.

Always be on the lookout for personal stories or situations that you can relate that will make folks laugh. Self-deprecating humor not only breaks the ice, but also shows your human side. It is a higher form of humor, because it takes confidence and insight to share your foibles with others. You will never have to worry about forgetting the details, either!

Collect Funny Stuff

Whether you like light or dark humor, make a point of collecting it at home and at work. Try collecting funny signs, e-mailed jokes, bumper stickers, comics, toys, hats, posters, costumes, and props. Use a journal or file to record stories, jokes, riddles, Freudian slips, malapropisms, puns, and oxymorons that make you chuckle. Keep it handy for instant comic relief.

Photographs can also be a source of inspiration. Slip into one of those photo booths in a shopping mall, draw the curtain, and make funny faces for a strip of "photofunnies." Doodle handlebar mustaches and devil horns on magazine photos of celebrities and politicians. Use Photoshop® to give yourself a beehive hairdo or a Las Vegas–style Elvis outfit.

Look for funny web sites. Some of our favorites include:

- www.chortler.com (a newsletter with "the cutting edge of erroneous news, inaccurate reporting and insight-free analysis")

- www.dribbleglass.com (jokes, pictures, billboards, trivia, cards—all funny)

- www.laugh.com (funny books, CDs, gifts, and more)

See Appendix B, page 122, for more humor web sites.

Go Fun Places With Fun People

Seek out people and places that make you laugh. Depending on where you live, there may be comedy clubs and events to experience locally. Consider going to the bigger laughter festivals such as Just for Laughs in Montreal, Canada. Now in its 23rd year, it draws 1.7 million spectators and 2,000 artists from around the world.

There are also more than 2,000 laughter clubs worldwide. Groups of people gather with a Certified Laughter Leader™ and laugh together using laughter exercises. These are organized by the World Laughter Tour, Inc., created by Steve Wilson, psychologist, president, and "Cheerman of the Bored." Members experience the contagious nature of laughter by using breathing exercises and exaggerated facial expressions. They learn how to laugh deeply and for a longer period of time—at nothing at all! Jokes and comedy are not needed—only people who want to laugh. Look for a local club on the World Laughter Tour web site (www.WorldlLaughterTour.com).

You may even try learning about therapeutic clowning as a way to explore and expand your sense of humor. Many hospitals (especially those for children) and nursing homes welcome clowns who bring joy and spontaneous humor to their patients and families. Clowns can minimize stress and help people heal. This special form of clowning is different from birthday-party clowning. Some places use volunteer (often called "caring") clowns, while others hire specially trained professional clowns. Blow bubbles, sing a little song, or simply listen with all your heart: You will lessen the patient's pain.

Keep It Clean

As educators, we know that taunting, violent, racist, sexist, and demeaning forms of humor are harmful and must be avoided. Reflect on the stories and jokes you tell, and screen them for appropriateness and sensitivity.

KEEP SMILING

It is normal to falter when you learn anything new, but do not give up. If you follow some simple guidelines, your sense of humor will expand, and your work and life will be enriched:

- Choose humor that suits your personality.

- Reconnect with your inner child.

- Use healing, nonhurtful humor.

- Tell personal stories. Learn to laugh at yourself more often.

- Open up your eyes and ears to the humor around you.

Points to Ponder

Anybody who has a normal mental development can engage in and benefit from humor. All they have to do is put themselves in this more playful state of mind. We have to give ourselves permission to do something we did very easily when we were 3 years old.
—John Morreal, president of Humorworks

What are some funny personal stories you could refine and tell?

What can you do today to start having more fun?

Chapter 4

Learning Through Humor: The Theory

True learning always takes place in a spirit of joy and abandonment.
—Maria Montessori, youth education pioneer

WHAT ARE YOUR FONDEST MEMORIES OF SCHOOL? Think back to your favorite teachers: They probably were good-natured and made you laugh. Teachers interested in their work show it naturally with their enthusiasm, smiles, and sense of humor. Students feel engaged by these teachers and are more willing to invest themselves in their own learning.

Remember the teacher who always did the unexpected, like teaching a lesson wearing horn-rimmed glasses, rubber nose, and moustache? How about the teacher who put students in groups and challenged them to build the tallest tower they could using only soda straws? Or the teacher who used games like Jeopardy!®, bingo, or Wheel of Fortune® to reinforce learning in mathematics or spelling? Teachers who challenge students and encourage their natural curiosity and problem-solving abilities greatly increase their motivation to learn.

Obviously, the primary role of the teacher is not to make students laugh, but to ensure that they learn. Teachers need to set and maintain high standards in order to teach the demanding curriculum required by state, federal, or provincial legislation. Humor, however, makes teaching and learning *easier*. Students who have been engaged by the material leave the classroom smiling with the day's lessons vivid in their minds. Having fun is not at all at odds with being a results-oriented, true learning community.

Geniality and lightheartedness set a positive social context in which teachers and students quickly build relationships. When laughter and learning coexist, an environment of trust, creativity, spontaneity, and joy is created. These are essential elements in every learning community.

WHY WE NEED THE HA-HA

Sometimes to get the "ah-ha" you need to have the "ha-ha"!
—Judy Siegel, writer

A sense of humor has been identified as a top characteristic of good classroom teachers: Students of teachers with a strong humor orientation tend to learn more in the classroom (Hudson, 1999). They describe their teachers as exceptional, motivating, enthusiastic, and playful. These educators are able to weave together the *science* of teaching (planning instruction and assessment, organizing, decision-making, and time management) with the *art* of teaching (creating the learning environment, role modeling, student advocacy, caring about students, and listening to parents). They see teaching not just as a job, but as a joyous calling.

Learning Benefits

In a classroom energized by laughter:

- Students become more motivated, alert, and attentive.

- Teachers and students feel more connected.

- Students learn faster and retain what they have learned over longer periods.

- Students are more willing to take risks because mistakes are portrayed as an acceptable, even fun part of the learning process.

Humor engages both sides of the brain and stimulates the creativity so essential to classroom teamwork and innovation. It encourages divergent thinking and problem-solving, builds self-esteem and confidence, and relieves boredom. The psychological distance between teachers and students breaks down, and even discipline becomes easier to manage.

Social Benefits

In a playful learning environment based on congeniality and respect:

- Students develop positive working relationships with the teacher and each other.

- Students are more likely to trust and confide in their teachers.

- Students learn lifelong social skills that can benefit their family, relationships, and career.

- Incidents of harassment and bullying may be defused.

Humor reduces tension, relieves stress, and improves morale. In this kind of positive, open environment, teachers get to know their students better—and the better we know our students, the better able we are to respond to their learning needs.

HOW STUDENTS LEARN

Students bring a wide variety of strengths and needs into the classroom each day. Responding effectively to this diversity is a great challenge. The decisions we make when we develop curricula, design student assessment strategies, choose teaching strategies, establish the classroom environment, and manage classroom behavior have a critical impact on student learning. But when we understand the principles of how students learn, we emerge from our own learning process better equipped to use humor and laughter strategically in our teaching.

Multiple Intelligences

Howard Gardner, a professor at the Harvard Graduate School of Education, challenged traditional beliefs in education that intelligence can be measured objectively and reduced to a single number or IQ score. In *Frames of Mind: The Theory of Multiple Intelligences* (1983), he argued that we define intelligence too narrowly. He proposed that human beings possess at least seven different intelligences (since revised to nine) that reflect different ways of interacting with the world.

THE NINE INTELLIGENCES

Linguistic—The capacity to use language to express yourself and understand others

Logical/Mathematical—The capacity to understand underlying principles or to manipulate numbers

Musical/Rhythmic—The ability to think in music or to hear patterns, recognize them, and manipulate them

Visual/Spatial—The ability to represent the spatial world in your mind

Bodily/Kinesthetic—The capacity to use your body to solve a problem, make something, or put on some kind of production

Interpersonal—The ability to understand other people

Intrapersonal—The ability to understand oneself

Naturalist—The ability to discriminate among living things; sensitivity to other features of the natural world

Existential—The ability and proclivity to pose and ponder questions about life, death, and ultimate realities

(Gardner, 1983)

Gardner suggests that each person possesses all nine intelligences in a unique combination much like a fingerprint—or a funprint! These intelligences work together in complex ways, and most people can develop each intelligence to an adequate level of competence. He concludes that there are many different ways to be smart within intelligences and between intelligences: All students are smart, but in different ways (Gardner, 1983).

Other kinds of intelligence have been proposed, including humor. Gardner does not consider humor a separate intelligence, however, but rather an element embedded in other intelligences. For example, humor shared between people may reflect interpersonal intelligence. When you enjoy a private laugh over something, you may be experiencing a benefit of intrapersonal intelligence. Laughing over something unexpected reveals logical intelligence.

Humor may also be embedded in other ways of being smart. Clever puns and word play by people like Ogden Nash, Victor Borge, and Snoop Dogg reveal their linguistic intelligence. Visual/spatial intelligence is an integral part of Chuck Jones' animation (Bugs Bunny) and of comic strips by cartoonists like Gary Larson (*The Far Side*) and Lynn Johnston (*For Better or For Worse*). The humor of Ray Stevens, P. D. K. Bach, Weird Al Yankovic, and Jack Black relies heavily on music intelligence, while the physical humor of Laurel and Hardy, the Marx Brothers, Carol Burnett, and Jim Carrey shows bodily/kinesthetic intelligence.

Teachers can increase their effectiveness by using information about multiple intelligences to create a classroom learning environment that appeals to all students. The intelligences are not static and can be learned. It is never too late to develop an intelligence, including the ones that involve humor.

Emotional Intelligence

In *Emotional Intelligence* (1997), psychologist Daniel Goleman extended Gardner's theory of multiple intelligences by expressing interpersonal and intrapersonal intelligences as five abilities.

One aspect of emotional intelligence is the concept of "social intelligence," the ability to understand others and act wisely in

---

EMOTIONAL INTELLIGENCE

Self-awareness—Knowing your emotions; recognizing feelings as they occur

Managing emotions—Handling feelings like fear, anxiety, anger, and sadness in appropriate ways

Self-motivation—Channeling emotions in the service of a goal; emotional self-control; delaying gratification and stifling impulses

Empathy—Sensitivity to the feelings and concerns of others

Managing relationships—Managing emotions in others; social competence and social skills

(Goleman, 1997)

---

human relations (Goleman, 1997, p. 42). The most critical element for student success in school, however, is an understanding of how to learn. Learning potential includes seven key ingredients:

1. **Confidence**—The child's belief that he or she is likely to succeed

2. **Curiosity**—The child's belief that learning is a good and pleasurable thing

3. **Intentionality**—The child's desire and ability to have an impact and to persist in that desire

4. **Self-control**—The child's ability to control his or her own actions (to the extent possible at his or her age)

5. **Relatedness**—The child's ability to understand and believe that he or she is understood by others

6. **Capacity to communicate**—The child's ability to verbally express and listen to ideas and feelings

7. **Ability to cooperate**—The child's ability to recognize that one's own needs must be balanced with those of the group (Goleman, 1997, p. 194)

The use of humor in the classroom directly correlates to and supports several of these key learning ingredients. In particular, humor stimulates curiosity by making learning fun. A light-hearted classroom atmosphere also builds trust and confidence. It increases the ability of children to relate to and engage with others in positive ways.

THE PLAYFUL CLASSROOM

Even though learning is serious business, a learning community can be a playful place. Business guru Tom Peters says that work must be fun: If it is dull and boring, he suggests, we are wasting our lives. The same principle applies to teaching: It should be fun, not a chore!

You may be afraid to look silly in front of your students. You may worry about losing control of your classroom. You may be concerned that humor or laughter in class will be viewed negatively by administrators who think that students who are having fun are not working and therefore not learning. Perhaps your strong work ethic keeps you from relaxing long enough to even consider using humor as a learning tool.

But we know that children, especially very young ones, love to laugh and have fun at whatever they do. Children are naturally curious and eager to learn and try new things. Their enthusiasm, imagination, and passion help make the classroom a playful place and teaching and learning fun.

Each year teachers face the challenge of creating a classroom environment that will allow students to grow and succeed. We are wise to capitalize on our students' enjoyment of laughter and fun to enhance the teaching and learning environment. Make a deliberate choice to be positive! An upbeat, enthusiastic outlook coupled with a sense of humor enables you and your students to travel the playful path to knowledge.

Creating a Safe Place to Learn

It is unfortunate that some new teachers are advised, as Paul was, "Never smile before Christmas." This teaching chestnut holds that if a new teacher appears too "soft" early in the academic year, students will "take over" the classroom. Despite this misguided advice, most first-time teachers are smiling and laughing with their students in very short order. They intuitively understand that smiling and laughter make learning possible, rather than impede it.

How can you use and encourage humor, keep control of the classroom, and ensure that learning takes place? The classroom is not a comedy club, nor should it be. Classroom humor must be combined with clear standards and expectations for acceptable work and behavior in a structured environment.

But a teacher cannot create an emotionally safe classroom by simply invoking arbitrary rules. All class members must *understand* the impact of their words and actions on others. Model positive forms of humor in your classroom to help students understand how to use humor to build a safe, fun learning environment for everyone. When your students explore their own humor, be sure to differentiate between the negative class clown and the whimsical class clown. The negative class clown is disturbing, distracting, or inappropriate; he or she makes the classroom tense. The whimsical class clown is funny and creative; he or she brings the classroom to life.

In a safe environment, students are able to ask for help, take risks, use their abilities, and learn to their potential. But as children get older and the stakes of learning get higher, fear of making a mistake or being the object of ridicule or judgment can interfere with the natural joy of learning. Students are reluctant to engage in the classroom when the classroom is a volatile, upsetting place. A student-teacher relationship characterized by laughter and warmth can replace fear with respect, trust, and a love of learning.

Building Relationships

Humor is not a cure-all. Think of it as a catalyst to improve the learning community for the students and the teaching environment for you. Humor helps to build relationships and support the cause of learning, but it does not work in a vacuum.

It is essential that you know your students well, including their names, interests, and family backgrounds. Each class and student has a unique personality. It is up to you to determine the kind of humor to use and how to adapt it to the greatest advantage. Young children enjoy silly humor such as clown noses and wigs. Junior high and high school students may feign indifference, but they still appreciate a sense of humor. Older students may be more responsive to cognitive or off-the-wall humor. Regardless of their age or level of sophistication, all students love to laugh.

USING HUMOR IN THE CLASSROOM

DO

- Relax, smile, and laugh with your students. Allow students to enjoy your presence and personality.

- Reveal your sense of humor. You will have the students' attention, and you will teach more effectively.

- Use self-deprecating humor. It is always safe since it is about you, not your students.

- Know your students well before deciding on the type and appropriateness of humor in your classroom.

- Capitalize on unexpected hilarious moments.

DON'T

- Say you do not have a sense of humor. Each of us has a unique sense of humor.

- Be afraid to use humor. Just remember that it may take practice.

- Worry about looking silly. Even if you do, chances are you will gain the esteem of your students rather than lose it.

- Use ridicule, cynicism, or sarcasm. These have a negative impact on relationships and do not improve learning.

- Expect humor to correct major student misbehavior or to cajole a deeply upset student. Find more appropriate means to deal with these situations.

The best news for teachers is that humor is a skill, not a gift, and like all skills, it can be learned and improved. Doing stand-up comedy in front of the class is not required! Humor may take the form of being playful or telling amusing anecdotes from your life. Just sharing some laughter and smiles with your students opens up communication and establishes rapport, essential tools for successful teaching. As you practice your humor, students soon learn that you have a life outside of the school and that you are human, even vulnerable—just like them.

It should go without saying that you should never use sexist, racist, hostile, biased, or sick humor in the classroom. Humor should enhance the classroom environment, not make students uncomfortable or distract from learning.

LEARN TO LAUGH

Research, experience, and common sense show that laughter and humor have a positive impact on the classroom learning community. Like any skill, a sense of humor can be learned and improves with practice. When laughter and humor are present in your classroom, students feel engaged and safe. Creativity, teamwork, and learning are sure to flourish. The next chapter will explore easy, practical ways you can begin to incorporate humor into your classroom and get your students laughing and learning.

Points to Ponder

In the new workplace, with its emphasis on flexibility, teams and a strong customer orientation . . . emotional competencies [are] becoming increasingly essential for excellence in every job and in every part of the world.
—Daniel Goleman, noted psychologist

How can you weave laughter and humor into your lessons to use and stimulate different kinds of intelligence?

Jot down a few funny, self-deprecating stories that you would feel comfortable sharing with your students.

Chapter 5

Learning Through Humor: The Practice

A smile is the shortest distance between two people.
—Victor Borge,
entertainer and humorist

WOULD YOU LIKE TO INCREASE YOUR EFFECTIVENESS with students, make the curriculum come alive, enhance your creativity and teaching skills, and bring more joy to your work? Well, you can! Laughter and a sense of fun in the classroom can improve student learning, reduce stress and discipline problems, and increase students' willingness to collaborate with one another and with you. Lighthearted fun in the classroom engages students and makes them feel confident enough to attempt new challenges.

This chapter offers practical ideas for increasing the humor and laughter in your classroom, enhancing the classroom climate, and improving the teaching and learning environment. Be open to your students' humor, encourage it, and the benefits will follow.

GIVE YOUR CLASSROOM A HUMOR TUNE-UP

Once you have decided to add more humor and laughter to your classroom, recommit to the idea daily. Getting started can be the most difficult part of making any change. Some strategies will become a habitual part of your teaching practice, and others will rotate in and out of your repertoire over time.

First Steps

Start by subtly introducing humor into the classroom's physical environment and daily routines.

- Post cartoons on a bulletin board or display colorful posters with lighthearted captions or funny quotations to set the stage for fun. Choose materials that suit your personality. Encourage students to put up their own items, too.

- Begin each day with something humorous—a quotation, top-10 list, pun, riddle, or story. Humorous anecdotes that connect to the curriculum or to a school event work best. Ask students to contribute.

- Openly share your own sense of humor with the students through signature items such as a favorite tie, scarf, or pair of socks. Use facial expressions, smile, and laugh often. Tell stories about yourself and your own blunders and frailties.

- Model for students that laughter is acceptable in the classroom. Most humor in the classroom is spontaneous, so watch for opportunities and take advantage of them.

- Encourage students to take a leadership role in making the classroom fun so that responsibility does not rest with you alone. Introduce a regular "humor time" into your daily agenda for students to share funny stories about things happening in their lives. Be sure to set clear parameters for what is acceptable and what is not. If your own sense of humor needs some fine-tuning, this is a great way to start introducing fun into the classroom.

- Establish a joy committee or humor club to create new ideas that will bring more laughter and good humor to the classroom. Reward students who contribute ideas with a handshake, a heartfelt "Thank you," a sticker, a certificate, or a smile. Even older students appreciate these gestures.

- Ask students to create a classroom mascot. The mascot can be real or imaginary: an animal, symbol, object, or cartoon. Use it to remind students that they can work together as a team to build a joyful, caring learning community.

Curriculum Strategies That Work

Creative classroom humor brings curriculum to life. *How* you teach is as important as *what* you teach. Good teaching is more than keeping the students awake or under control. By incorporating some laughter and humor into your teaching repertoire, you can capture the students' attention, motivation, and curiosity for learning—in any subject.

- In a biology class, paint a large heart on butcher paper and place it on the floor. Have students walk through it to follow the route the blood takes as it circulates through arteries and veins. Play pulsing drum music in the background.

- In a mathematics class, use a bingo sheet to help students practice calculating and finding correct answers.

- In a language arts class, lighten up vocabulary lessons with oxymorons like "hot chili," "lampshade," "work party," and "jumbo shrimp." Ask students to think of Tom Swifties like "'I need a pencil sharpener,' Tom said bluntly." Play with palindromes. Include simple ones like "madam" and "radar" as well as more complex versions like "A man, a plan, a canal—Panama!" (See www.fun-with-words.com for more.)

You can use many creative and unique methods to teach or review concepts, regardless of the subject area or grade level. Use your imagination!

- Role-playing, rap songs, song parodies, chants, trivia, students-as-teachers, and improvisation reinforce learning and help students remember ideas and facts in preparation for assessment.

- Games such as Wheel of Fortune, Jeopardy!, and spelling bees are novel and stimulating for students and improve retention.

- Keep an age-appropriate collection of joke books, computer games, puzzles, and board games in your classroom. These can be used to reinforce learning and stimulate creative thinking and problem-solving. They can also be used as incentives for some students to complete their work and for others to reward a job well done.

- At the beginning of a unit, tell a story, pose a riddle, or play a game that captures student interest and connects their prior knowledge and experience to the new concept or information. To introduce the class to the mechanics of punctuation, for example, start by playing Victor Borge's "verbal punctuation" by making sounds in place of periods, question marks, and exclamation points. Read a funny poem that fits in to the unit you are going to teach. Try poems by Shel Silverstein from one of his anthologies for children or by Kenn Nesbitt from his web site (www.poetry4kids.com).

- Incorporate the unexpected into your lessons (October is National Pizza Month; April 15 is Rubber Eraser Day). Use humorous stories, puns, jokes, and riddles as literacy exercises for the students.

- Give students who are naturally funny an opportunity to recap a lesson. The presenting students enjoy the attention, and the rest of the class enjoys the presentation. When used appropriately, this technique gives students a simple opportunity for classroom leadership and gives you another opportunity to assess whether the essential facts and skills have been presented and understood.

- As part of oral language development, have a "best joke" contest, or ask students to deliver a 1-minute impromptu speech or comedy routine to the class. Award silly prizes to the participants (clown noses, bubble gum, gummy bears, Hawaiian leis, noisemakers, kazoos, tiaras, or crowns).

- Collect some well-known proverbs, give students the first half of each proverb, and ask them to complete the sayings in their own words. Here are some examples:

    Strike while the . . . bug is close.

    The pen is mightier than the . . . pigs.

    Where there's smoke, there's . . . pollution.

- As part of thoughtful, well-planned lessons, incorporate humorous, appropriate clips from television shows and movies that reinforce the curriculum and portray real-life situations that students will relate to and remember.

- Take students on field trips. Field trips are a powerful way to reinforce learning, enhance the curriculum, and create a common learning experience. They are also fun!

Remember to group students in various combinations (alone, in pairs, in small groups) so that they learn to work successfully in different team settings and gain experience speaking in front of small and large groups. This allows students to develop self-confidence and teaches them to collaborate more spontaneously as part of daily learning.

Assessment Strategies That Reduce Tension

There is a growing need for educators to infuse humor and laughter into assessment periods and tasks. Students feel the stress of testing because they know the impact the results can have on their futures. Used appropriately, humor enables students to remain focused and positive and achieve their best results. Humor and laughter increase adrenaline, oxygen flow, and pulse rate.

After these heightened responses, students actually become more relaxed and calm, and test results can improve.

- Be enthusiastic, humorous, and positive when you give your students assessment feedback. Both positive verbal feedback ("Correct!" "Great!" "Close!" "Super!") and non-verbal encouragement (smiles, nods, and gestures) help keep students focused on their learning and aware of their progress.

- Give corrective feedback *during* learning (formative assessment) rather than suspending judgment to the end (summative assessment). Let students learn from mistakes before it is too late; you will reduce their stress and show them that mistakes are part of learning. Students, especially perfectionists, need to know that everyone makes mistakes and that an honest mistake should not lead to feelings of anger, depression, or shame. Teachers can model resilience by deliberately or inadvertently making mistakes in front of their students. If students can laugh at their own errors, they can quickly move past them and continue learning with no emotional turmoil.

- Place humorous cartoons or multiple-choice questions on tests. Add funny bonus questions at the end of the test (riddles, brain teasers, word jumbles, crosswords, word searches, or anagrams). A mathematics bonus question might ask, "How much dirt is in a hole measuring 6 x 8 x 9 feet?" The correct answer is none, of course, as there is no dirt in a hole!

- Make story problems funny. For example, a physics teacher can ask how much force a donut thrown out of a car window at a certain speed would have if it hit a student waiting at a bus stop.

- Help students relax before a test or exam. Show them a funny cartoon, allow them to bring in their good-luck charms, and lead a discussion about different ways they can handle stress, remain composed, and do their best.

TEACH HUMOR

Teaching students about humor and its usefulness and benefits should be an essential part of the curriculum at all grade levels. Students need to understand the significance of humor at school or work, in friendships, in family life, and in personal growth.

- Have younger students research their family's funny personal stories and practice telling one of them to the class with appropriate props.

- Ask older students to investigate any aspect of humor in the media: newspapers, magazines, television, commercials, and in movies. They could also research their favorite comedians or humor theorists. Students can design a collage or do an oral presentation for the class to represent their findings.

- Pose a series of questions to students about the nature of humor and discuss their answers either as a whole class or in small groups. The age of the students will determine the types of questions asked and expected depth of the discussion. Here are a few possible topics:

- Why do different people find different things funny?
- Is it a good thing that people laugh? Why?
- Does laughter make us feel better in any way? How?
- What does "funny" mean?
- What makes the funniest person you know funny?
- What makes the funniest movie you have seen funny?

- Ask students of all ages to rate how happy they feel on a 10-point scale and to write down their responses. Then show them excerpts of a funny movie and ask them to rate themselves again. Their feeling of happiness should improve from their initial rating. Have students write a journal entry in which they try to explain the significance of the results.

LAUGH TO LEARN

Humor can be used to enhance your classroom environment, enliven the curriculum, and reduce student stress during evaluation. When students learn about humor in all its forms, they become aware of its usefulness and impact, and are able to use it more effectively in their own lives. If you are committed to incorporating more humor into your teaching, your students are already benefiting from your decision. Taking even small incremental steps will create a more dynamic and vibrant classroom learning community.

Points to Ponder

What would you attempt to do if you knew you could not fail?

—Robert Schiller, writer

What aspect of your curriculum do students most dread, and how can you use humor to teach it more effectively?

List five steps you will take to incorporate more humor into your teaching.

Part 3
The Leader's Role in Creating a Collaborative School Culture

Chapter 6

Leading With Humor: The Theory

A sense of humor is part of the art of leadership, of getting along with people, of getting things done.
—Dwight D. Eisenhower, former United States president

WE AGREE WITH THE PROPONENTS of the professional learning communities movement that responsibility for school leadership does not rest solely on the principal. The principal may be the leader of leaders, but leadership resides in the whole school—not just with those who hold formal positions of power.

Teachers hold key leadership positions, as the previous chapter showed. They have significant opportunity and power to motivate, inspire, and transform the lives of both students and colleagues. But administrators are also well-positioned to make unique and lasting contributions to the lives of students, teachers, and the school as a whole. In fact, every member of the school community has leadership potential, including staff, students, and parents.

Why lead with laughter? Laughter is the lubricant that can help leaders build a professional learning community. Leadership without laughter and humor can be tedious and uninspiring for all parties. Leaders who see the lighter side of work and of themselves find leading enjoyable and rewarding—and are more readily accepted and appreciated by others.

Michael Kerr, humorist and author, argues that humor:

- Improves the learning environment and service to students

- Boosts morale and motivates staff

- Reduces stress, employee turnover, and absenteeism rates

- Improves trust and eases communication

- Facilitates change

- Strengthens relationships and teamwork

- Enables leaders to manage with a lighter touch (Kerr, 2004b)

In schools, our "clients" reward us with smiles every day. Schools by their very nature are vital, fun places. Effective leaders know that laughter and good humor are essential components in setting and maintaining a positive school tone, and they capitalize on the energy of humor and laughter to improve learning and the quality of school life.

INSPIRATIONAL LEADERSHIP

Hunter "Patch" Adams is a doctor and social activist who has devoted his life to changing the healthcare system by championing the use of laughter and humor in mainstream medicine. Adams' approach to patient care can best be described as "whatever works" to make people feel better about themselves and their situation. He enjoys making people laugh and teaches doctors how to be funny for their patients because he considers laughter and joy to be an integral part of treatment and healing.

Patch Adams combined his work as a physician with his skills as a therapeutic clown to bring his sense of humor and message of hope to people around the world. In a commentary on the movie about his life, the real Patch Adams says that "working hard to make the world a better place is fun to do and not a sacrifice . . . but a jubilant thrill to help others" (Shadyac, 1998).

Educational leaders share many of the traits that are ascribed to therapeutic clowns. How many of the following descriptors are characteristic of your leadership style?

- Vulnerability
- Intuitiveness
- Attentiveness
- Trustworthiness
- Honesty
- Humility

- Patience
- Gentleness
- Kindness
- Playfulness
- Curiosity
- Imagination

- Compassion
- Acceptance
- Inclusiveness
- Empathy
  (Hospital for Sick Children, 2005)

The principles applied in hospitals by Patch Adams are just as relevant in our schools. Teachers look to leaders for inspiration in good times and bad. Humor and laughter fuel their optimism and motivation, and the ultimate beneficiaries are the students.

Why Humor Works

A joyous mood is infectious and brings success. Intimidation may achieve something momentarily, but not for all time. On the other hand, when hearts are won by friendliness they will take on all hardships willingly, so great is the power of joy over people.

—Hexagram 58, "The Joyous," *I Ching*

Some leaders believe that laughter in school wastes time and diminishes productivity. On the contrary, leaders who encourage laughter and humor help others feel less overwhelmed and more capable. A playful approach also helps people enjoy their work, feel more in control of their day, and be more positive about their students and colleagues. Laughter and humor create a bond between and among the administrators and teachers. Just as teachers who use humor appropriately are better liked and respected by their students, so, too, are administrators.

As Michael Kerr tells us:

Putting humor to work isn't about people standing around the water cooler exchanging one-liners. Having a sense of humor is about having a sense of perspective and *using the ability* to find humor in situations to manage stress and creatively problem solve. Adding humor is about *celebrating* work, not trivializing it. And it's about mixing humor in an *appropriate* manner to improve workplace productivity. (Kerr, 2004a, italics original)

Humor helps schools release energy and creativity and counteracts teacher isolation, resistance to change, and conflict. Laughter also helps staff members open their minds to new ideas about their work. Humor and laughter are not a panacea. But when they are combined with genuine appreciation and praise, they can help teachers become more productive, trusting, loyal, and willing to work collaboratively. Trust and loyalty are not created by a paycheck; they are nurtured by strong relationships with colleagues and a caring, supportive principal.

If your school has no history or culture of fun and laughter, you may have to initiate structured fun until people catch on. A student pep rally, a motivational speaker, or an after-school social event in place of a meeting are good ways to start on an institutional level, but the best way to start is by changing your own attitude.

Overcoming Doubt and Fear

If you are hesitant about incorporating humor at work because you fear failure, keep in mind that humor allows us to laugh at our weaknesses, gaffes, and eccentricities in a positive and nourishing way.

People will need time to get to know you and your sense of fun. Introduce humor gradually, pay attention to others' reactions, and tweak your humor as needed. In the workplace, as we have mentioned, one of the safest and best ways to begin to incorporate humor is to poke fun at yourself: Admit your mistakes, and let go of your ego.

Trying to safeguard your credibility by concealing your sense of humor may cause you to be seen as too self-important. Conversely, too much joking around can cause you to be perceived as someone who never takes anything seriously. Use humor with discretion so that you earn respect as well as affection. Get to know your audience, and respect the limits of your school's culture.

SCHOOL CULTURES

Roland Barth's *Improving Schools From Within* (1990) remains a critical book on school culture. In it, he pinpoints key issues of school culture that are still being discussed today: empowering teachers, implementing and sustaining change, and encouraging communication, collegiality, and risk-taking among adults to create a "community of learners."

Barth suggests a reason for the rise in adversarial and competitive relationships and professional isolation in schools:

> I believe these problems are rooted in the relationship between teacher and principal. I have found no characteristic of a good school more pervasive than a healthy teacher/principal relationship. It models what all relationships will be. What needs to be improved about schools is their culture, the quality of interpersonal relationships and the nature and quality of learning experiences. . . . A key to improving schools from within lies in improving the interactions among teachers and between teachers and principals. (Barth, 1990, p. 19)

School culture refers to the beliefs that are valued and the expectations that operate in a school, particularly in relationships. Simply stated, culture is the way we relate to each other: "the way we do things around here."

Six Models of School Culture

Marvin Wideen, a retired faculty of education professor from Simon Fraser University in Burnaby, British Columbia, Canada, identifies six types of school culture (Wideen, 1994). Each culture is determined by the personal and work interactions that occur. The six cultures represent a continuum from worst- to best-case scenario (see chart on page 80).

Take time to reflect on and assess the culture and interactions in your grade, department, school, or district. Keep in mind that a school can have subcultures that yield very different results from the overall school culture.

The most difficult transition for a school is moving from "nice neighbors" to "harmonious community." In this shift, the amount of commitment, hard work, and anxiety rises substantially. As a school moves toward "the good school" and "super school" levels, it focuses primarily on work interactions that are collaborative and dynamic.

Paul Spies (2003) notes that even being a member of a dysfunctional team is better than the professional isolation that comes from having no team at all:

> Many teams' biggest challenge is learning to work with colleagues for a common purpose, but collegial effort is also a catalyst for continual professional development. Exposing to your colleagues what you can do as a teacher and how you do it stretches you and can lead to personal and professional reflection. . . .
>
> When I first began team teaching on a four-person team . . . I was motivated to leave the social studies hallway and venture

SIX MODELS OF SCHOOL CULTURE

	Personal Interaction	Work Interaction
1. Little Shop of Horrors	Loneliness and distrust prevail. There is constant friction and open hostility. Outbursts are common.	Staff behave unprofessionally. Teachers isolate themselves for protection and hoard supplies.
2. Egg Carton	People get along but are a little distant and cautious.	Departments are balkanized, and administrators are disengaged.
3. Nice Neighbors	People work hard to have a friendly school. There are many parties, games, and food rituals.	Teachers still work alone, but they acknowledge one another's strengths. Isolation takes the guise of professionalism.
4. Harmonious Community	The school climate is friendly. People talk about their personal lives *and* their teaching.	A community of leaders begins to form. Teachers talk positively about teaching and students. Staff begin to work collectively toward a common goal.
5. The Good School	The entire staff is collegial. They collaborate, trust, and care for one another. Support staff are included and valued as part of the community. There is time for reflection and solitude. Success is celebrated.	Voluntary collaboration (in study groups, teams, and observation) is the norm. Teachers experiment, take risks, and practice interactive professionalism.

6. The Super School
This is the "Good School" with something extra: a "take on the world" attitude and a constant striving for excellence. Winning is expected. Personal and work interactions merge, with impressive results. All educators want to experience this culture at least once.

(Adapted from Wideen, 1994)

into other areas of the building. It always amused me when colleagues in other departments either kindly or jokingly asked, "Are you lost? Can I help you?"

. . . Despite evidence that teaming can have a positive impact on teacher and student attitudes, performance and growth, high schools and teachers resist teaming. They may fear scheduling conflicts, personality conflicts and losing control. . . .

I've participated on largely dysfunctional and even somewhat stressful teams, but they were still better than being isolated as a teacher because our students formed a community and I knew exactly who their other teachers were. (Spies, 2003, pp. 58–61)

Collaborating with others is your opportunity to make a contribution and to make a difference. This is a powerful message that we cannot ignore.

The Professional Learning Community

In *Getting Started: Reculturing Schools to Become Professional Learning Communities* (Eaker, DuFour, & DuFour, 2002), the authors emphasize that changing the school culture to a professional learning community is difficult, takes time, is nonlinear, and requires a collaborative culture.

In the first three types of culture discussed earlier, there is very little positive work interaction, which is the primary determinant of a professional learning community. To create change, a leader must state unequivocally to his or her staff that collaboration is not an option, but an expectation. Collaboration by invitation does not work (Eaker, DuFour, & DuFour, 2002).

Positive changes in the culture begin once the systems and routines that require people to work together are created and embedded in the daily practices of the school. One strategy is to establish collaborative teams that work interdependently to achieve common goals for student learning. As teachers become less isolated, they begin to enjoy some of the benefits of working together, including less time spent planning and better results from students. By working together, educators achieve what one person cannot accomplish alone.

What does humor have to do with school culture and leadership? Humor and laughter can play a significant role in the initiation and development of the collaborative culture so essential to a professional learning community.

If your school is a "little shop of horrors," it will be evident in the staff's dominant type of humor—if there is any. Cynicism, sarcasm, and demeaning remarks will be common.

When the school culture begins to move toward "nice neighbors," staff members become friendlier and therefore more willing to participate in celebrations, rituals, and shared events—but only on a personal level. In this culture, everyone gets along over a shared meal, but when the bell rings, the classroom doors close, and each teacher is on his or her own. It takes a lot of time and energy to make the changes necessary to get to the next level.

True teamwork begins once a school moves toward becoming a professional learning community. At that point, leaders can introduce humor strategies into professional development meetings to help staff face the challenges of school improvement and internalize humor as a core school value.

Even after a school achieves "super school" characteristics, its leaders must not become complacent. Vigilance and maintenance are required. School culture needs to be nurtured every day by the behavior and attitudes of the staff and the students, the choices they make, and how they treat each other.

Consider creating an interdisciplinary committee of staff, parents, and students to act as guardians of the school mission. The committee can monitor the school culture and give a kind of "state of the union" address once each term to show how the school's words are demonstrated by the community's actions. Is the school doing what it says it does? Do the programs and daily interactions reflect the school vision, mission, values, and goals? Use formative assessment on your school's performance: Adjust your practices before failure becomes unavoidable.

Humor in the Mission, Vision, Values, and Goals

The best school cultures are founded on collaboratively developed and shared statements. In order to progress, school staff must answer these questions:

- **Mission**—Why do we exist?

- **Vision**—What kind of school do we want to become?

- **Values**—How must we behave in order to become the kind of school we hope to be?

- **Goals**—What steps are we going to take, and when will we take them? (Eaker, DuFour, & DuFour, 2002, pp. 12–18)

The answers to these questions form the basis of all decisions that guide the school.

Take time to create and include statements about the place of humor and laughter in the school vision, mission, values, and goals. Humor and laughter can also serve as catalysts in the process of collaboration. Include elements of humor in creating ideas for a school mascot, cheer, motto, or school song.

BE A POSITIVE ROLE MODEL

If you are interested in improving your school's culture by adding more humor and fun to the organization, keep these pointers in mind:

- Be yourself. Do what feels comfortable.

- Keep it simple. Small daily efforts make a difference.

- Be relevant. Humor that focuses on the school, department, or division works best. A school bonds around humorous shared experiences.

- Hire for humor. In interviews, look for people who have an upbeat approach to life and a sense of humor. Your staff will benefit, and collaboration will be enhanced.

- Give yourself and others permission to play. People look to school leaders to set the tone. You can choose to be a catalyst for creativity and energy.

- Keep things in balance. Do not lose sight of your most important roles as instructional leader, role model, and supervisor.

The role of the leader in a professional learning community is to promote, protect, and defend the school vision and values, and to inspire and motivate others (Eaker, DuFour, & DuFour, 2002, p. 29). A sense of humor is one of the most undervalued, underappreciated, and underutilized human resources in achieving these goals. Each of us can be a leader in the school community. Adding humor and laughter to our workday and relationships will aid all of us in our quest to create schools that can take on the world.

Points to Ponder

There are two ways of spreading light: to be the candle or the mirror that reflects it.

—Edith Wharton,
Pulitzer Prize–winning American novelist

How can you use humor to strengthen the culture of your school?

List some specific ways you can motivate and encourage school teams to work more interdependently to achieve school goals.

Chapter 7

Leading With Humor: The Practice

If we couldn't laugh, we would all go insane.
—Jimmy Buffett, musician

LAUGHTER AT WORK IS OFTEN SEEN AS UNIMPORTANT or even inappropriate, but it is a constructive force integral to a productive working environment. Keeping up with changing curriculum requirements, new discipline procedures, and lengthy school improvement processes can be exhausting for overworked teachers and staff, but good leaders find ways to keep everyone inspired when the going gets tough. Working together need not be a chore! Humor can be the glue that binds a diverse group of educators together and makes it a joy to serve others.

Laughter and humor are strongly linked to lifelong learning, but many administrators and educators do not currently recognize their importance. Leaders in a learning community have a special responsibility to address that deficit, as their language and behavior set the standard for others to follow. Make it your personal mission to do whatever you can to cultivate laughter in your learning community. Commit yourself to living each day with joy and passion as a model for those you hope to lead.

This chapter provides some "fun-damentals" that we have used as leaders to increase the laughs per day and bring staff and students closer together in our schools. Feel free to choose from this menu of options to feed your school's unique hunger for fun.

START WITH YOURSELF

Ask yourself, "How much fun am I to be with at work?" If you are uncertain, ask your colleagues. Whether you are a Dry Wit or a Soft Touch, share your unique humor style and temperament with your staff and students. Polish up your sunny smile, goofy laugh, clever puns, sly grin, or fun-loving, cheerful disposition. By giving yourself permission to laugh, play, and have fun at work, you give others permission as well. Laughter is infectious!

- On the way to or from school, listen to a funny tape or CD while driving.

- At school, smile frequently. Look for opportunities to laugh.

- Spend more time with humorous, fun-loving people. Ask a funny colleague out for lunch.

- Always be ready to laugh at yourself, so that you do not leave that job exclusively to others.

- Find your smile "triggers," and incorporate more of them into your day. Your trigger may be a cartoon, a funny joke, or just personal contact with kids. Make fun part of your daily routine!

- Take a break during the day to think about something that really makes you laugh—a movie, a joke, or a funny incident.

- At the end of the day, mentally review funny moments that you can retell later.

RAMP UP THE FUN

The best laughter is usually spontaneous. Keep new humor initiatives short, simple, and lighthearted. Create an environment that promotes fun!

- Begin each day on a positive note. Purchase a laugh track or a sound effects CD to add some fun to the morning announcements on the public address system.

- As part of the morning announcements, include a thought for the day, a tongue twister, an unfinished joke, or an unanswered question of the day. Encourage students to submit punch lines for the joke or answers to the riddle. Give prizes for the best submissions: Wax lips, yo-yos, candy necklaces, Silly Putty®, Tootsie Rolls®, and plastic Hawaiian leis work particularly well in elementary school.

- Play upbeat music in the school hallway. Ask students to suggest or contribute music that makes them happy or energizes them, and then play it at the beginning and end of the day or during the lunch hour.

- Create a "Wall of Fame" photo gallery in the main hall to highlight the achievements of students and staff and to recognize contributions made to laughter and fun. Encourage staff members and students to nominate others.

- Develop a humor section in the library. Include joke and cartoon collections as well as books, tapes, CDs, videos, and DVDs about humor, creativity, health, and wellness.

With Students

Becoming a principal or other administrator means relinquishing your influence in the classroom. In exchange, however, you receive an opportunity to influence the students and teachers in an entire school. A new principal quickly realizes that his or her relationship with the students has changed and become more distant: Students often think you have "crossed over to the dark side"! You can build a new relationship with students, but you have to work much harder and in different ways to succeed.

Make spending time with students a priority. Be there to greet them as they arrive and to say goodbye as they head home. Visit classrooms, go outdoors at recess and lunch, and lead cocurricular activities. By being there, you can connect with the students, learn their names and something about them, and build a new kind of relationship—the principal-student relationship. The students also have an opportunity to get to know you in a friendlier, more accessible context than your office.

Share your sense of humor with students: This is your chance to destroy some myths about principals! The commitment you make to students will have a powerful effect on the school climate. The laughter and lighter moments you share can help you reach some of the most difficult, unhappy, and isolated students. When students realize that the principal and staff care deeply about them, they feel more secure, more engaged at school, and more invested in their education.

- Invite students to participate in the creation of a school motto, song, dance, cheer, or mascot. Make these an important part of student assemblies. Sing, dance, or cheer along with the students!

- Hold regularly scheduled assemblies to share good news, celebrate achievements, present awards, and build school spirit. Encourage student and staff participation, and invite parents to attend.

- At assemblies, ask student volunteers to tell a joke or a funny story or speak for 1 minute about a topic of personal interest. Singing, dancing, playing the piano, or performing in a rock band builds the confidence of the performers and the school spirit of the audience. Performances must be strictly voluntary, and an atmosphere of mutual trust and respect between and among students and staff is essential.

- Organize a student talent show to celebrate the end of a term or school year. Hold auditions, and have a panel of staff members and students select the performers. Strive to include variety in performances such as singing, playing a musical instrument, dancing, stand-up comedy or comedic skits, one-act plays, and recitations.

- Arrange special all-school presentations by motivational speakers, musicians, and comedy and drama groups.

- In elementary schools, organize students into cross-grade teams and have a school-wide noncompetitive play day. Alternately, teach students how to play four square, wall ball, and skipping games at recess. Play a game or two yourself!

- Schedule regular theme or school spirit days. Ask students for their suggestions, and participate in the day's activities yourself. Try themes such as:

  - Beach Day

  - Twins Day

  - Backwards Day

  - Favorite Storybook Character Day

  - Neon Colors Day

  - Funny Hat Day

- Offer students cocurricular activities other than team sports. Unusual activities will appeal to a wider range of student interests. A Lego® or Barbie® club may work well in elementary school. For older students, offer nontraditional choices such as hiking, culinary, video, or community volunteer clubs in addition to a wide range of music, drama, academic competitions, and athletic activities.

- Consider starting a comedy club for students. You may nurture the comedic talents of the next Robin Williams!

- Arrange a few occasions each year for students and staff to mix socially—a picnic, barbecue, ball game, or skating or bowling outing.

- Encourage teachers to integrate field trips to fun locations (a science center, concert, or an outdoor education center) into the curriculum.

With Staff Members

Before people can function effectively as a team, they need to feel that they know each other. Because laughter is affirming and inclusive, experiences that create laughter and fun for everyone will help to open up lines of communication, boost staff morale, and create the cohesion that builds a strong learning community.

The school administration can and should share responsibility for injecting laughter into work. The work will be lighter and the results more fun for everyone.

- Give morale a boost by establishing a Joy Committee or "Giggle Squad" to take charge of special events like theme or school spirit days. Ask the staff and students to suggest activities.

- Form a laughter club for school staff that meets every morning for breathing, stretching, and laughter exercises.

- Organize a staff kazoo band or glee club, and take part in public performances.

- Create opportunities for people to get together at lunch or after work. Plan a range of activities that allow everyone to participate. Include physical activities like skating, miniature golf, bowling, hula-hoops, and Twister® contests as well as more sedate events like barbecues, movie nights, dinner boat cruises, and Monopoly® or darts tournaments.

- Hold a school-wide contest to match staff members to their baby pictures. Include your own picture!

- Create a secret buddy system to perform "random acts of fun" for one another (for example, during the week leading up to Valentine's Day, or on Groundhog Day). Have a "meet your secret buddy" party at the end of the time period.

- Encourage staff members to think of small ways to make one another smile—a cartoon in someone's mailbox, an apple on his or her desk with a thoughtful note, a birthday card—and set the example by doing it yourself.

- Invite former and retired staff members and school board personnel to special occasions such as student assemblies, theme days, and staff luncheons.

- Send a bouquet of "Hour Flowers" to a staff member with a note that says: "Enjoy these flowers for 1 hour, and then send them on to someone else you think may need them."

- During very busy or stressful times, such as reporting periods or standardized student testing, hire a professional masseuse for a day to provide staff members with free shoulder and neck massages.

- Host a laughter film festival at lunchtime or after school. Funny movie clips or short comedies of 30 minutes or less work best. For something different, try a laughter audio festival with comedy tapes or CDs. Serve popcorn!

- Make sure to express your appreciation to those very special staff members blessed with a great sense of humor and a willingness to share it.

In the Faculty Lounge

The faculty lounge is an oasis for staff members—a stress-free zone. Try to make the room less clinical and office-like and more personal and comfortable. Any of the following ideas will help generate the right atmosphere.

- Establish rotating teams to bring in simple snacks for everyone once a week on "Treat Day."

- Create an annual "unauthorized" yearbook of school highlights complete with fun photos, memorable moments, top-10 lists, significant dates and events, staff quotable quotes, and teacher trivia.

- Have the school photographer take two different staff group photos—an official one and a second one just for fun using props, costumes, and other humorous gear.

- Keep a communal photo album or scrapbook.

- Start a communal journal of funny things that staff members have heard or experienced in the school. Share the stories at staff meetings, parent nights, student assemblies, and in the staff bulletin or school newsletter.

- Keep a box of toys and props that are not only fun to play with, but also promote relaxation and creativity. Silly Putty®, Koosh® balls, windup toys, Etch A Sketch®, and a Magic 8-Ball® are an excellent start.

- Establish a collection of humorous articles, books, tapes, CDs, videos, and DVDs appropriate for teachers and staff, and encourage everyone to contribute to and enjoy these materials.

THE ROLE OF HUMOR IN DIFFICULT TIMES

Comedy is tragedy plus time.

—Carol Burnett, comedian

When schools experience difficult times, humor is temporarily displaced by grief: Tears, hugs, or simple words of encouragement replace laughter. Eventually, humor returns to help us take the sting out of that harsh reality. Through laughter, we release nervous tension and pent-up emotions and regain our perspective, balance, and optimism.

Colin Mochrie, star of *Whose Line Is It Anyway?,* explains:

> *I think you can almost make fun of anything—it becomes sort of a survival tactic. I've known people who have faced terminal diseases and after a certain amount of time they treat it lightly and make jokes that you could never make. . . . When you go through bad times a good laugh can cure an awful lot. . . .it's amazing how healthy you feel after a good laugh. (as quoted in Doyle Driedger, 2003, pp. 40–41)*

When difficult circumstances arise, look for opportunities that can help to lighten the moment, however briefly or gently. Your colleagues will be both appreciative and relieved. Remember how easy it can be to offend someone in pain with an ill-advised joke or inappropriate, careless remark. Use your best judgment, exercise some restraint, and apply a light touch. Be sure that your expression will be seen as timely, caring, and supportive.

In Your Office

When you become an administrator, your office communicates subtle messages about you, your expectations, and your priorities. Make it a cheerful, welcoming, well-organized place that serves as a model to others. The décor should reflect your interests, your personality, and your great sense of humor.

- Set up your computer screen saver with funny cartoons or quotations.

- Post a funny door sign that lets visitors know how warm and approachable you really are.

- Display humorous posters, pictures, and props around the room.

- Add a humor section to your bulletin board with cartoons, jokes, and quotes of the week.

- Have several candy jars on your desk and keep them filled for staff, students, and visitors.

- Keep a supply of funny stickers, self-stick notes, and thank-you cards for the unexpected. Use them in your communications with staff, students, and parents.

- Maintain a master calendar with birthdays, milestones, and other significant dates. Find small ways to celebrate these with others.

At Meetings

Meetings must be productive; people need to see the benefits of working together. If you plan to brainstorm, problem-solve, or work on school goals at a meeting or professional development session, humor will relax participants and open up communication. Laughter is motivating and encourages participation! The local discount store, toy store, and party store are great sources of fun, inexpensive toys, prizes, costumes, and props.

- Hold meetings off-site or in new locations within the school.

- Create agendas that include catchy titles, jokes, cartoons, and quotes.

- Give fun, inexpensive prizes at every meeting for First to Arrive, Best New Idea, Funniest Story, Best Behaved, Best Team, or other categories.

- Charge latecomers a fun penalty such as a quarter to the coffee or social fund.

- Change the routine of your meeting by including amusing anecdotes and accounts of current happenings. Encourage people to share their best work-related story, joke, or blooper.

- Add a timed "whine and cheese" item to the agenda. Encourage attendees to whine in a dramatic and exaggerated fashion about school issues.

- Make sure that you have simple treats (healthy or decadent) at every meeting.

- Add some pizzazz to transparency and PowerPoint presentations with funny inserts between slides of dry subject material.

- Use toys or props to loosen people up and spark creativity before planning or brainstorming sessions. For example, consult a Magic 8-Ball to answer staff questions.

- Add a "rumor mill" to the end of each meeting to quash rumors and get issues and concerns on the table safely.

- Instead of the usual meeting, watch an inspirational movie. Bring lots of popcorn and a few boxes of tissues!

- For a quicker, more productive meeting, try a stand-up get-together with no chairs.

- Call a "Fun Raising" meeting to brainstorm on ways to include more laughter and fun.

In Staff Bulletins

A regular bulletin helps keep everyone current and can add a great deal to the laughter and fun in the school. Invite staff to contribute!

- Include cartoons, funny anecdotes, top-10 lists, and quotations about laughter, learning, and fun.

- Recognize staff members in a fun or serious way.

- Communicate good news.

- Incorporate a week-at-a-glance calendar that acknowledges staff birthdays, milestones, awards, accomplishments, and other special occasions.

- Focus periodically on such things as wellness information, stress-reduction strategies, or recipes for healthy eating.

- Establish top 10–list themes, and ask staff to submit items such as "the top 10 reasons for not submitting report card marks on time."

In Celebrations

Rituals and ceremonies buoy spirits, bring people together, renew team energy and motivation, and promote values that the school considers important. Celebrations should commemorate the accomplishments of individuals as well as groups in academic and nonacademic areas. Take every opportunity to celebrate the contributions and achievements of staff members and students.

Use celebrations to say thank you, provide recognition, and show appreciation. Not all celebrations have to be milestones. They should also recognize improvement and effort, not just attainment of an arbitrary standard. Sometimes you may celebrate just getting through the day. Find ways to celebrate small but significant breakthroughs.

- Hold special staff awards ceremonies several times a year, particularly during stressful times. Include serious and playful awards. Awards suggested by other staff members are always highly prized.

- Instead of showing appreciation with applause, "give a toot" on a set of kazoos.

- Create fun team awards to promote collaboration.

- Dedicate a day to a specific group. For example, celebrate Administrative Professionals' Day, Boss Day, or Teacher Recognition Day. Remember to celebrate and thank the other important but often underappreciated school staff members, including bus drivers, crossing guards, care-takers, and cafeteria staff.

- Celebrate birthdays and other special events by serenad-ing the staff member with musical instruments or a makeshift staff choir.

Having trouble finding something to celebrate? Every day of the calendar year celebrates something, so keep a few of these in mind for celebration emergencies:

- January 30—Fun at Work Day
- February—Boost Your Self-Esteem Month
- April 1—Laugh at Work Week
- May 16—National Sea Monkey Day
- May 21—Bike to Work Day
- June 14—World Juggling Day
- September 19—Talk Like a Pirate Day
- October 27—Cranky Coworkers Day
- November 29—Electronic Greetings Day

In the Community

A school that exemplifies a collaborative culture is always looking for new ways to share its achievements. A good leader encourages and supports students and teachers to go beyond the school walls to celebrate their successes and serve others in the community.

- When fundraising with colleagues for philanthropic organizations such as the Heart Fund, the United Way, or the Cancer Society, create a list of inexpensive fun prizes or services that staff can win.

- When fundraising for the school, try something different from the usual candy sale. You may find students, staff, parents, and corporate sponsors are more enthusiastic about a walk-a-thon, dance-a-thon, or read-a-thon.

- Encourage student participation in community outreach projects such as a food drive or fundraising or disaster relief efforts. Add to the laughter and fun by offering prizes such as a pizza lunch or ice-cream social to motivate and reward the class making the biggest contribution.

- Ask students or staff members to bring some laughter to senior citizens by visiting senior centers and nursing homes. A lively performance by a school choir, band, or drama club can make an enjoyable contribution to the lives of seniors. Students will benefit from the extra practice needed for performance, from an increased understanding of older generations, and from new friendships that may result.

- Collaborate with local organizations to offer a wider range of after-school programs that help students and parents see the school in a new perspective. Consider offering a course for parents on ways to have fun with their teenagers. Students may enjoy courses in first-aid, babysitting, or clowning.

EXPLORE THE POSSIBILITIES

Still looking for even more ways to use humor to create a collaborative school culture? A simple Google search using the phrase "fun at work" yielded 199 million hits, and "laughter at work" resulted in 15.3 million hits! There are countless ways you can make working together more fun and productive. Decide what will work best for you, and begin or continue to add to the laughter and fun in your learning community.

Points to Ponder

Strange when you come to think of it, that all of the countless folk who have lived before our time on this planet, not one is known in history or in legend to have died of laughter.

—Sir Max Beerbohm, English essayist, caricaturist, and parodist

What can you do to renew your energy and creativity and bring a fresh commitment to your work as a leader?

Select three "fun-damentals" from this chapter that you will implement in your school this year.

Chapter 8

Professional Development With a Smile

*To love what you do and feel
that it matters—how could
anything be more fun?*
—Katherine Graham,
long-time publisher
of the *Washington Post*

NOT THAT LONG AGO, SCHOOL SYSTEMS CONSIDERED one day sufficient for their teachers' professional development needs for an entire year! Today, however, educational organizations realize that for real growth and change to occur, teachers need time to reflect, to experiment, and to collaborate with their peers.

Most school districts now provide a continuum of learning opportunities for educators, including induction and mentoring for beginning teachers, ongoing study groups, and periodic workshops. Many school leaders allocate weekly or even daily time and money to ensure that their teachers have opportunities to meet with one another, access educational expertise, and hone their skills. And because educators understand that none of our professional development efforts are justified unless they improve student behavior, knowledge, and skills, schools increasingly use data collection and analysis to measure the success of their programs.

School leaders must recognize that their staff will only accept and commit to professional learning and growth if certain realities are acknowledged at the outset:

- Since every school is unique, staff members must be involved in the design of a site-based plan for professional development.

- Creative activities bring the content to life.

- Staff must be treated with respect.

This chapter will show you how to address those realities by using humor to motivate and inspire your staff to move the learning community forward and create a super school with a "take on the world" culture.

INVOLVE STAFF IN PLANNING AND LEADING

The most forward-thinking districts approach professional development by asking each staff member to develop a plan that outlines what he or she needs personally to grow as an educator. Administrators then collect the plans, look for similarities, and use the data to design group learning activities targeted to address specific needs that staff members have identified.

Too often, however, districts issue a cattle call for professional development and only offer "Sit and Git" sessions in which all participants receive the same treatment regardless of their individual needs. There is nothing worse than feeling like professional development is being "done to you" without your input or collaboration. In that kind of coercive environment, professional growth will be minimal.

Share the process of designing, planning, and evaluating staff meetings and group activities with a team of staff members. If only one person is responsible for each stage of the process, he or she will find it hard enough to organize everything, let alone be creative. A team of several people can provide insight into the strengths and needs of their colleagues and can use their teaching and leadership skills to build more effective professional development sessions. This design team can then gather feedback after the session to help improve the next session.

UNLEASH YOUR CREATIVITY

In our consulting work with educators, we have often asked members of the audience to act out how teachers feel when they are herded into a room and "injected" with information from a visiting expert (see Sharma, 1982). We provide props and encourage participants to ham up their portrayals. Before long, we hear chuckles and see knowing nods around the room. As the relevance of the story to their own experience sinks in, the teachers become eager to participate in a lively discussion about how inservice topics are selected and which resource people are invited to a school or school district.

This is only one illustration of how you can use humor and a playful approach to hook the attention of your staff and overcome their preconceived notions and bad experiences with certain issues. Ask your planning team to find other creative, funny ways to engage staff members at the beginning of a planning session and get them motivated and alert.

Balancing content and process is a difficult juggling act. A professional development session should capture participants' attention, give them an incentive to learn, and meet the needs of various staff learning styles. It should provide meaningful information as well as opportunities to practice new skills and discuss creative alternatives and solutions.

Start by defining the content that the session should teach. Once you know the desired outcomes, inventing fun activities to facilitate open discussion and deepen understanding will become easier. Some of our favorites follow.

Use Cooperative Learning Strategies

Many cooperative learning strategies are ideal for adults as well as students. Experiment with small groups to involve the introverts. In "Think Pair Share," participants are given time first to reflect individually, then to talk with a partner, and finally to share with the whole group. This is quite an improvement from the Socratic technique of asking the whole group a question and calling on the first hand that pops up. Or use a "Jigsaw" method to make sure everyone is included and responsible for a piece of the task: Divide the whole group into subgroups and then assign one part of a task to each person. Each person then shares his or her work with their larger group.

Get Them Out of Their Seats

Getting participants up and moving honors the kinesthetic learning style and usually gives them a chance to talk—something all teachers need. Consider using these techniques:

- **Carousel Brainstorming**—Write questions on flip charts and have small groups move from one chart to another, adding their ideas. Debrief the results.

- **Stick 'Em Up**—Write questions as above, but have participants write their responses on sticky notes (one idea per note) and post them on the flip charts. Debrief the results.

- **Give and Get**—Have participants stand and exchange one idea with one person at a time. Each then moves on to another partner.

- **Help Line**—Seat participants in two lines facing each other. Each person poses a question or dilemma to the person opposite him or her, who then provides clarification and possible strategies. For example, if the topic is classroom discipline, one person will ask a question or describe a discipline situation that he or she is currently facing, and the partner will suggest possible strategies to deal with it. Reverse roles after several rotations.

Act Out the Goose Story

This story illustrates the benefits of teamwork by showing why geese fly in a V formation and how they encourage each other (see Appendix C, page 125). Bring fun props such as hats or wings, and ask for seven to nine volunteers to act as a flock of geese. Read the story step by step, and coach them through it the first time. Then let them "fly solo" and act out the story on their own.

Take time afterwards to help the group make the connections between a flock of geese and a collaborative school culture. Discuss how this activity might be shared with students in a classroom learning community. Pass out copies of the story for everyone to take home.

Show Movies

Consider showing movies or short film or television clips that illustrate the point you want to make in an amusing way. If you use an excerpt, give staff a brief description of the plot up to that point and indicate what you want them to watch for.

The *I Love Lucy* episode called "Job Switching" often prompts a good discussion. In this episode, Lucy and Ethel get jobs working on an assembly line in a candy factory. Their supervisor instructs them that they do not have the option of pausing the assembly line and in fact will have to go faster and faster as they get used to the system. Lucy and Ethel inevitably fall behind, but rather than simply calling for help, they attempt their own complicated, comical solutions.

Ask your staff members to consider and discuss the parallels between an assembly-line "career" and teaching. How do they perceive the supervisor in the episode and her treatment of the workers? Who caused the ultimate problem? What appeared to be evidence of a job well done? What should have been evidence?

We have also achieved good results from showing a segment from the movie *Sister Act.* In this clip, Whoopi Goldberg's character, Deloris, takes over a choir from a nun who has run it for years and is somewhat resentful of being replaced. Deloris takes stock of where the choir is as a group, assesses the strengths of individual choir members, and then assigns each a role that capitalizes on those strengths. She manages to win over the retiring choirmaster by asking for her opinions. She is kind but firm with her "students," emphasizing to them that they will only improve as a choir if they work together and practice, practice, practice.

Ask your staff to consider and discuss the parallels between the choir and a school with regard to the importance of teamwork and leadership. How does a good leader interact with team members? How can team members serve as leaders within the group?

You may find new ways to use these particular examples in your professional development sessions, or you can choose your own film clips. Remember to select lighthearted, enjoyable material that makes people laugh!

TREAT STAFF MEMBERS WITH RESPECT

Adult learners have several specific characteristics: They need to have their opinions, experience, and expertise respected and valued, and they need opportunities to converse and share knowledge. Most importantly, they need what they are studying to clearly address their needs. Keep these characteristics in mind as you plan a professional development session.

If the only opportunity for a professional development meeting is at the end of the school day, remember that people have worked a full day and often face more work at home; use this time with care and respect. Make sure the session does not waste their precious time. Good food and hot coffee are always welcome. Allow some initial time for folks to mingle socially and catch up with each other. Try to build in some levity even though the subject may be serious. Plan carefully, but be flexible, always allowing time for staff members to talk with and listen to one another—and to laugh.

PLAN ON LAUGHING

Professional development is a crucial component of any school's journey to excellence. But taking a lighthearted approach to certain aspects of professional development does not at all undercut its importance. In fact, planning for laughter increases the likelihood that you will make an impact on hearts as well as minds. If you have a leading role in professional development, exchange ideas from your laughter repertoire with other educators so that you can develop your own treasure chest of alternative strategies. Collaboration starts with a smile!

Points to Ponder

To be playful and serious at the same time is possible, and it defines the ideal mental condition.
—John Dewey, 19th-century philosopher and educational theorist

How would you respond to staff members who think laughter at meetings is frivolous?

Write down some suggestions to make the format of an upcoming meeting more fun.

A FEW JOKES FOR THE ROAD

To get some feedback from my grade 10 students during my first year of teaching, I asked them to answer a short teacher-evaluation questionnaire I had prepared. One question was "What do you like best about this teacher?" An answer of note was "Her red shoes."

—Ellen West, Truru, Nova Scotia
(© 2000 by Reader's Digest Magazines Limited. Reprinted by permission from the September 2000 issue of *Reader's Digest*.)

The question on a test I had given to my grade 8 students read: "Find x: x + 17 = 32." On a technicality, however, I had to mark one confused student's answer correct: He had found and carefully drawn a circle around x.

—Donna Bell, Quesnel, British Columbia
(© 1999 by Reader's Digest Magazines Limited. Reprinted by permission from the November 1999 issue of *Reader's Digest*.)

For a French assignment, we had to read a French novel, write a report about the book and present it orally. In class, our teacher chose one of my classmates, notorious for not doing assignments, to answer questions about characters, places and descriptions. He had her convinced he had read all 400 pages of the novel until he blew it—by summing up his presentation with ". . . and that's how the movie ended."

—T. Webster, Niagara Falls, Ontario
(© 1999 by Reader's Digest Magazines Limited. Reprinted by permission from the November 1999 issue of *Reader's Digest*.)

The Last Laugh

*Among those whom I like, I can
find no common denominator;
but among those that I love, I
can: All of them make me laugh.*
—W. H. Auden,
poet

WE HOPE WE HAVE MADE STRONG ARGUMENTS for the importance of consciously incorporating laughter and fun into the everyday culture of the learning community. We think humor has been sorely lacking in the minds and practices of many educators.

If you are a new teacher, be yourself in the classroom. Share your personality and sense of humor with your students. Start with the curriculum you are assigned to teach, and strive to teach it with creativity and a smile. Find small ways to bring laughter into the classroom, and build from there.

If you are an experienced teacher, think about adding at least one new humor strategy to your repertoire. Review and refine some of your old fun techniques. Encourage your principal and other teacher-leaders to add some zip to the school culture by trying one of our suggestions, or offer to take responsibility for leading the change yourself.

If you are a principal, seek out staff and students who are blessed with a sense of humor and encourage them to use this skill and intelligence. You have a huge influence on everyone with whom you interact. Share the real you, and have fun at work. Although your job is full of serious responsibilities, you can approach it with a positive attitude.

If you are a central office consultant or superintendent, remember that even though you are physically removed from schools and students, you have a great deal of influence on school culture and tone. Think about how you can apply the ideas in this book to:

- New teacher training and pre-service

- Principals' courses

- Mentoring of new principals, assistant principals, and teachers

- Curriculum writing

- Selection of texts and audiovisual resources

- Professional development initiatives

- Allocation of budget for resources and learning

We challenge you and all of our readers to reach beyond your comfort zone and take a chance. Make increasing the laughter level in your school and in your life a priority, and develop an action plan that allows you to start small and think big. Begin with the changes you want to see in yourself, and make a commitment to those. Do not let the people and forces that are beyond your control hamper your resolve or enthusiasm. Talk with others, and share the message that *laughing matters.*

When you try the ideas and suggestions in this book, please let us know how they turn out. We would also love to hear about any other humor strategies you have heard about, experienced, or used yourself to enhance student learning, build a more joyful learning community, or make professional development more fun and effective. We look forward to learning and laughing with you!

Appendix A

LaughLAB Jokes

The following jokes are reprinted for your enjoyment from LaughLAB *(2002), with permission from the British Association for the Advancement of Science.*

Best Joke as of December 2001

Sherlock Holmes and Dr. Watson were going camping. They pitched their tent under the stars and went to sleep. Sometime in the middle of the night Holmes woke Watson up and said: "Watson, look up at the stars, and tell me what you see."

Watson replied: "I see millions and millions of stars."

Holmes said: "And what do you deduce from that?"

Watson replied: "Well. If there are millions of stars, and if even a few of those have planets, it's quite likely there are some planets like Earth out there. And if there are a few planets like Earth out there, there might also be life."

And Holmes said: "Watson, you idiot, it means that somebody stole our tent."

The Top Doctor Joke

The doctor gives the patient a check-up and looks very concerned.

Patient: "Okay doc, break it to me, how long do I have to live?"

Doctor: "Ten."

Patient: "Ten what? Years? Months?"

Doctor: " . . . nine . . . eight . . . seven . . . six . . ."

The Winning Science Joke

Two atoms were talking. One atom said to the other: "Why are you crying?"

The atom replied: "I've lost an electron."

The first atom said: "Are you sure?"

"Yes," replied the other. "I'm positive."

Top Joke as Voted by People Aged 11–15

A new teacher was trying to make use of her psychology courses. She started the class by saying: "Everyone who thinks they're stupid, stand up!" After a few seconds, Little Johnny stood up.

The teacher said: "Do you think you're stupid, Little Johnny?"

Little Johnny replied: "No ma'am, but I hate to see you standing there all by yourself."

Appendix B

Additional Resources

PRINT RESOURCES

Adams, P. (with Mylander, M.). (1993). *Gesundheit!* Rochester, VT: Healing Arts Press.

Armstrong, T. (1994). *Multiple intelligences in the classroom.* Alexandria, VA: Association for Supervision and Curriculum Development.

Burgess, R. (2000). *Laughing lessons: 149⅔ ways to make teaching and learning fun.* Minneapolis, MN: Free Spirit.

Feigelson, S. (1998). *Energize your meetings with laughter.* Alexandria, VA: Association for Supervision and Curriculum Development.

Goleman, D. (2000). *Working with emotional intelligence.* New York: Bantam.

Hemsath, D. (2001). *301 more ways to have fun at work.* San Francisco: Berrett-Koehler.

Hoffer Gittell, J. (2003). *The Southwest Airlines way: Using the power of relationships to achieve high performance.* New York: McGraw-Hill.

Klein, A. (1989). *The healing power of humor: Techniques for getting through loss, setbacks, upsets, disappointments, difficulties, trials, tribulations, and all that not-so-funny stuff.* Los Angeles: J. P. Tarcher.

LaRoche, L. (2001). *Life is not a stress rehearsal.* New York: Broadway Books.

Leno, J. (2005). *How to be the funniest kid in the whole wide world (or just in your class).* New York: Simon & Schuster Books for Young Readers.

Lundin, S., Paul, H., & Christensen, J. (2000). *Fish! A remarkable way to boost morale and improve results.* New York: Hyperion.

Lundin, S., Paul, H., & Christensen, J. (2003). *Fish! Sticks.* New York: Hyperion.

Lundin, S., Paul, H., & Christensen, J. (2004). *Fish! For life.* New York: Hyperion.

Ravich, L. (2002). *A funny thing happened on the way to enlightenment.* New Orleans/Metairie, LA: Gestalt Institute Press.

Shade, R. (1996). *License to laugh: Humor in the classroom.* Englewood, CO: Teachers Idea Press.

Tamblyn, D. (2003). *Laugh and learn: 95 ways to use humor for more effective teaching and training.* New York: Amacom.

Weinstein, M. (1996). *Managing to have fun.* New York: Simon & Schuster.

Wooten, P. (1996). *Compassionate laughter: Jest for your health.* Salt Lake City, UT: Commune-A-Key.

ELECTRONIC RESOURCES

Humor Advocates and Speakers

Don Gascon: www.humorforyourhealth.com

Loretta LaRoche: www.stressed.com

Michael Kerr: www.mikekerr.com

The HUMOR Project, Inc.: www.HumorProject.com

Steve Wilson's World Laughter Tour: www.worldlaughtertour.com

Organizations Promoting Humor for Health

Association for Applied and Therapeutic Humor: www.aath.org

Canadian Association of Therapeutic Humour: www.canadahumour.org

Hospital Clown Newsletter: www.hospitalclown.com

Laughter Club International (Dr. Kataria's School of Laughter Yoga): www.laughteryoga.org

Martin Seligman's Reflective Happiness Program: www.reflectivehappiness.com

Patch Adams' Gesundheit! Institute: www.patchadams.org

Personality Tests and Profiles

Personality Dimensions from Career/Life Skills Resources, Inc.: www.clsr.ca

David Keirsey's Temperament Sorter: www.keirsey.com

Personality types for professional type practitioners: www.16types.com

True Colors: www.truecolors.org

Products and Jokes

Books, CDs, gifts and more: www.laugh.com

Canadiana Connection: www.canadianhumour.com

Directory of free humor web sites: www.100topjokesites.com

Jokes, pictures, billboards, trivia, cards: www.dribbleglass.com

Kenn Nesbitt's poetry for children: www.poetry4kids.com

Satirical online newspaper: www.chortler.com

Wordplay: www.fun-with-words.com

ENTERTAINMENT RESOURCES

Comedians With Funny Audio CDs, Videos, and DVDs

Woody Allen	Dennis Miller
Victor Borge	Mike Nichols and Elaine May
George Carlin	Gilda Radner
Johnny Carson	Chris Rock
Dave Chappelle	Jerry Seinfeld
Bill Cosby	Lily Tomlin
Steve Martin	Robin Williams

Movies

Ace Ventura	*Monty Python and the Holy Grail*
As Good As It Gets	*Mrs. Doubtfire*
Bruce Almighty	*The Nutty Professor*
Fargo	*The School of Rock*
A Fish Called Wanda	*Shrek*
Good Morning, Vietnam	*Some Like It Hot*
I Love Lucy	*The Terminal*
Legally Blonde	*Tootsie*
M*A*S*H*	*What About Bob?*

Appendix C

The Goose Story

The following story by Dr. Harry Clark Noyes is reprinted from ARCS News, 7(1), January, 1992, with permission from AIDS Related Community Services. Try acting it out in your professional development sessions to demonstrate the importance of teamwork (see page 109).

Next fall, when you see geese heading south for the winter, flying along in V formation, you might consider what science has discovered as to why they fly that way: As each bird flaps its wings, it creates an uplift for the bird immediately following. By flying in a V formation, the whole flock adds at least 71% greater flying range than if each bird flew on its own.

Lesson: *People who share a common direction and sense of community can get where they are going more quickly and easily because they are traveling on the thrust of one another.*

When a goose falls out of formation, it suddenly feels the drag and resistance of trying to go it alone and quickly gets back into formation to take advantage of the lifting power of the bird in front.

Lesson: *If we have as much sense as a goose, we will stay in formation with those who are headed the same way we are.*

When the head goose gets tired, it rotates back in the wing, and another goose flies point.

Lesson: *It is sensible to take turns doing demanding jobs with people or with geese flying south.*

Geese honk from behind to encourage those up front to keep up their speed.

Lesson: *What do we say when we honk from behind?*

Finally, and this is important, when a goose gets sick, or is wounded by gunshots and falls out of formation, two other geese fall out with that goose and follow it down to lend help and protection. They stay with it until it is able to fly, or until it dies. Only then do they launch out on their own, or with another formation to catch up with their group.

Lesson: *If we have the sense of a goose, we will stand by each other.*

References

Barth, R. (1990). *Improving schools from within: Teachers, parents, and principals can make the difference.* San Francisco: Jossey-Bass.

Beck, M. (2002, May). The clue is in your funprint. *O, The Oprah Magazine,* 223–227.

Beck, M. (2003). *The joy diet: Ten practices for a happier life.* New York: Crown.

Berens, L. (2000). *Understanding yourself and others: An introduction to temperament.* Huntington Beach, CA: Telos.

British Association for the Advancement of Science. (2002). *LaughLAB: The scientific quest for the world's funniest joke.* London: Arrow Books.

Cousins, N. (1979). *Anatomy of an illness as perceived by the patient: Reflections on healing and regeneration.* New York: Norton.

Doskoch, P. (1996, July/August). Happily ever laughter. *Psychology Today, 29,* 33–35.

Doyle Driedger, S. (2003, April 21). People really want to laugh. *Maclean's, 116,* 40–41.

Eaker, R., DuFour, R., & DuFour, R. (2002). *Getting started: Reculturing schools to become professional learning communities.* Bloomington, IN: Solution Tree (formerly National Educational Service).

Feinsilber, M., & Mead, W. (1980). *American averages: Amazing facts about everyday life.* Garden City, NY: Doubleday.

Gardner, H. (1983). *Frames of mind: The theory of multiple intelligences.* New York: Basic Books.

Garner, J. (2004). *Made you laugh: The funniest moments in radio, television, stand-up, and movie comedy.* Kansas City, MO: Andrews McMeel.

Gascon, D. (2002). *The humor for your health guidebook.* Calgary, Alberta, Canada: Humor for Your Health™.

Goleman, D. (1997). *Emotional intelligence: Why it can matter more than IQ.* New York: Bantam.

Hospital for Sick Children. (2005). What is a therapeutic clown? Toronto, Ontario, Canada. Available at www.sickkids.on.ca (retrieved February 6, 2006).

Hudson, D. (1999, August 19). Prescription for learning. *News-Courier* (Atlanta, AL).

Kataria, M. (1999). *Laugh for no reason.* Mumbai, India: Madhuri International.

Keirsey, D., & Bates, M. (1978). *Please understand me: Character and temperament types.* (3rd ed.). Del Mar, CA: Prometheus Nemesis.

Kerr, M. (2004a). Managing to have fun. Available at www.mikekerr.com (retrieved December 28, 2005).

Kerr, M. (2004b). Why we need to put humor to work. Available at www.mikekerr.com (retrieved February 3, 2006).

Kerr, M. (2004c). Why work stress is a laughing matter. Available at www.mikekerr.com (retrieved December 15, 2005).

Klein, A. (2003a). A hearty laugh, a healthy heart. Available at www.allenklein.com/articles (retrieved February 2, 2006).

Klein, A. (2003b). Laughter and humor: Myths and realities. Available at www.allenklein.com/articles (retrieved February 2, 2006).

LaRoche, L. (2003). *Life is short—wear your party pants: Ten simple truths that lead to an amazing life.* Carlsbad, CA: Hay House.

Loma Linda University School of Medicine. (1999, March). Laughter research conducted at LLUMC. *Loma Linda University School of Medicine News.* Loma Linda, CA: Author.

Loomans, D., & Kolberg, K. (1993). *The laughing classroom: Everyone's guide to teaching with humor and play.* Tiburon, CA: H J Kramer.

McGee-Cooper, A. (1990). *You don't have to go home from work exhausted! The energy engineering approach.* Dallas: Bowen & Rogers.

Mitchell, C., & Sackney, L. (2000). *Profound improvement: Building capacity for a learning community.* Lisse, the Netherlands: Swets & Zeitlinger.

Peck, M. S. (1987). *The different drum: Community making and peace.* New York: Simon & Schuster.

Philips, E. (1999). The classification of smile patterns. *Journal of the Canadian Dental Association, 65*(5), 252–254. Available at www.cda-adc.ca/jcda/vol-65/issue-5/252.html (retrieved December 13, 2005).

Provine, R. (2000, November/December). The science of laughter. *Psychology Today, 33,* 58–63.

Puder, C. (2003, August). The healthful effects of laughter. *International Child and Youth Care Network CYC-Online, 55.* Available at www.cyc-net.org/cyc-online/cycol-0803-humour.html (retrieved February 6, 2006).

Seligman, M. (2002). *Authentic happiness: Using the new positive psychology to fulfill your potential for lasting fulfillment.* New York: Free Press.

Shade, R. (1996). *License to laugh: Humor in the classroom.* Englewood, CO: Teacher Ideas.

Shadyac, T. (Director). (1998). *The medicinal value of laughter* [Documentary]. In *Patch Adams: Collector's Edition DVD.* United States: MCA Home Video.

Sharma, T. (1982, February). Inservicing the teachers: A pastoral tale with a moral. *Phi Delta Kappan, 63*(6), 403.

Spies, P. (2003, Summer). Promised land or assembly line? *Journal of Staff Development, 24*(3), 57–63.

Wallis, C. (2005, January 17). The new science of happiness. *Time, 165,* 40–47.

Wideen, M. (1994). *Struggle for change: The story of one school.* London: Falmer Press.

About the Authors

SUSAN STEPHENSON

Sue was "reinvented," as she says, when she retired a few years ago as a principal and returned to being a staff developer. She has had a varied career in elementary and secondary schools and in central office leadership roles. She is an award-winning presenter and lives in Brampton, Ontario, Canada, with her husband, Tom. She is a stepgrandmother with a passion for laughing, creativity, and Staples, her favorite store.

PAUL THIBAULT

Paul is a retired educator with more than 35 years of service, including work as a staff developer, principal, and director of principal qualification programs. His leadership, knowledge, enthusiasm, and sense of humor have won him the trust and respect of others.

Paul lives in Mississauga, Ontario, Canada, with his wife, Sharyn, and has two sons. The other joys in his life include friends, Beethoven, travel, and fast cars.

Paul and Sue collaborate in their speaking and consulting company, TNT Associates (www.tntassociates.ca). They can be reached at 905-453-9178 in Canada.

Make the Most of Your
Professional Development Investment

Let Solution Tree (formerly National Educational Service) schedule time for you and your staff with leading practitioners in the areas of:

- **Professional Learning Communities** with Richard DuFour, Robert Eaker, Rebecca DuFour, and associates
- **Effective Schools** with associates of Larry Lezotte
- **Assessment *for* Learning** with Rick Stiggins and associates
- **Classroom Management** with Lee Canter and associates
- **Crisis Management and Response** with Cheri Lovre
- **Discipline With Dignity** with Richard Curwin and Allen Mendler
- **PASSport to Success** (parental involvement) with Vickie Burt
- **Peacemakers** (violence prevention) with Jeremy Shapiro

Additional presentations are available in the following areas:

- At-Risk Youth Issues
- Bullying Prevention/Teasing and Harassment
- Team Building and Collaborative Teams
- Data Collection and Analysis
- Embracing Diversity
- Literacy Development
- Motivating Techniques for Staff and Students

Solution Tree
304 West Kirkwood Avenue
Bloomington, IN 47404-5131
(812) 336-7700
(800) 733-6786 (toll free)
FAX (812) 336-7790
e-mail: info@solution-tree.com
www.solution-tree.com

NEED MORE COPIES OR ADDITIONAL RESOURCES ON THIS TOPIC?

Need more copies of this book? Want your own copy? Need additional resources on this topic? If so, you can order additional materials by using this form or by calling us toll free at (800) 733-6786 or (812) 336-7700. Or you can order by FAX at (812) 336-7790, or visit our web site at www.solution-tree.com.

Title	Price*	Quantity	Total
Laughing Matters	$ 9.95		
Building Classroom Communities	9.95		
Getting Started	19.95		
The Handbook for SMART School Teams (book and CD-ROM)	54.95		
Harbors of Hope	21.95		
On Common Ground	29.95		
Passion and Persistence (video)	24.95		
The Power of SMART Goals	24.95		
Teaching Empathy (book and music CD)	34.95		
Through New Eyes (video)	174.95		
		SUBTOTAL	
		SHIPPING	
Continental U.S.: Please add 6% of order total.			
Outside continental U.S.: Please add 8% of order total.			
		HANDLING	
Continental U.S.: Please add $4. Outside continental U.S.: Please add $6.			
		TOTAL (U.S. funds)	

*Price subject to change without notice.

❏ Check enclosed ❏ Purchase order enclosed

❏ Money order ❏ VISA, MasterCard, Discover, or American Express (circle one)

Credit Card No._____ Exp. Date_____
Cardholder Signature _____

SHIP TO:

First Name_____ Last Name _____
Position _____
Institution Name_____
Address _____
City_____ State_____ ZIP _____
Phone_____ FAX _____
E-mail _____

Solution Tree (formerly National Educational Service)
304 West Kirkwood Avenue
Bloomington, IN 47404-5131
(812) 336-7700 • (800) 733-6786 (toll free) • FAX (812) 336-7790
e-mail: orders@solution-tree.com • www.solution-tree.com